ACKNOWLEDGEMENTS

Writing a book is a difficult project that requires a lot of patience and perseverance. I have been fortunate to have had the help of the following people who made the task that much easier. My sincere thanks are extended to everyone who helped in completing this project:

First, my family, for putting up with me when I needed to come home and lick my wounds.

Rochelle Mazzone, Claude Argyll, Wendy Hay, Lisa Thomas Himmer, Marilyn Purdhom, and Debbie Heffron, for reviewing the manuscript and providing me with valuable feedback. Dugan Pulsipher of First Interstate Bank / Reno for his advice in the financial areas, and Patty Jones of Foxfire Apartments / Reno for her advice regarding apartment rentals.

Holly Kondras for all her help and suggestions throughout this project. You are a class act, Holly!

Eric and Maria Clothier for being great friends and helping to make this book possible.

Special thanks to David Morgan for steering me in the right direction and for the valuable feedback on this manuscript.

A round of applause for Jim Roderick of the University of Nevada - Reno for editing and taking me through the book line by line to show me how I could make the final product the best it could be. Thanks to John Ellis for copy editing the book and making sure I dotted all my i's and crossed all my t's.

In addition, the creative work done by Lynn Wilton (cover illustration) and Susan Keyser of Skoosh Ink (cover design) is also greatly appreciated.

v

DISCLAIMER

This book is written and intended to be used as a guide only. The publisher and author are not engaged in the profession of rendering any form of legal or accounting advice. If for any reason legal or accounting advice is necessary you should seek out qualified professionals.

The purpose of this book is to educate and acquaint anyone with the desire to live on their own with practices and principles that may help them to achieve that desire without having to learn everything by making mistakes.

Every effort has been made to provide complete and accurate information on this subject. Please send requests for additional information to Richardson Publishing. If possible, such requests will be answered in future editions of this book.

The author and Richardson Publishing shall have neither liability nor responsibility to any person or entity with respect to any loss or damage caused or alleged to be caused directly or indirectly by the information contained in this book.

Young *people* *...* *...ready* *to* *strike out on their own will find* *Feeney's unpretentious* *text* *appealing and will welcome the op...* *...* *...* *...* *...* *...* *...asing a tough transitio...*

...KLIST

Now here's a book for all ages. Feeney has put together in a humorous manner a checklist of needed reality factors. Like Alexander's sword through the Gordian Knot, Feeney's guide helps you to make a clean break.

> *- Milton T. Wolf / Acquisitions Librarian*
> *University of Nevada / Reno*

As a college instructor teaching freshman courses I often see my students in the throes of being away from home for the first time, and sadly, their unpreparedness on the home front hinders their progress in school. Both set of stress can combine to really put the kids on the hot seat.

I feel your tips and wonderful anecdotes will prove a valuable resource to those who take the time to acquaint themselves with your suggestions. Your book should probably be required reading in freshman courses.

> *- Jim Roderick / Instructor of English*
> *University of Nevada / Reno*

The humorous yet common sense approach to life's obstacles make "So You Want To Move Out?" a perfect book for anyone moving out for the first time.

> *- Dugan Pulsipher / Vice President*
> *First Interstate Bank / Reno*

SO YOU WANT TO MOVE OUT?

A GUIDE TO LIVING ON YOUR OWN

BY
RIK FEENEY

RICHARDSON PUBLISHING

SO YOU WANT TO MOVE OUT?
A Guide To Living On Your Own
by Rik Feeney

RICHARDSON PUBLISHING
3983 South McCarran Boulevard
Suite 412
Reno, NV 89502

Library of Congress Catalog Card Number   93-90442
ISBN # 0-9637991-0-X

Publisher's Cataloging in Publication
(Prepared by Quality Books Inc.)

Feeney, Rik, 1958-
   So you want to move out?: a guide to living on your own / by Rik Feeney.
   p. cm.
   Includes bibliographical references.
   Preassigned LCCN: 93-90442.
   ISBN 0-9637991-0-X
   1. Single people--United States--Life skills guides. 2. Living alone--United States. 3.Moving, Household. 4. Home economics.
I. Title.

HQ800.F44 1994   305.9'0852
                                      QBI94-97

Credits:

Cover Illustration by Lynn Wilton
Cover Design By Susan Keyser of Skoosh Ink

CONTENTS

Introduction:

"Success is to be measured not so much by the position that one has reached in life, as by the obstacles which he has overcome while trying to succeed."

-Booker T. Washington

INTRODUCTION

Because of my profession, I have had the opportunity to live in many parts of the world. In each new place, I needed to find an apartment, furnish it, find new friends, develop a budget for living on my own, and generally go about enjoying life as best I could. I think I have been successful, however, there are several lessons I learned the *hard way*. In other words, each lesson cost me a lot of money. You don't forget lessons like that. Fortunately, I could return home to lick my wounds whenever I made a serious mistake.

Within this book, I will explain how anyone with proper planning can set up their own place to live, meet their bills, furnish their home comfortably, and enjoy life on their own terms.

Whether this is the first time you are setting up a place to call your own, or the first time in a long time, you need to review the basics. This book will cover all the basics needed to make it on your own.

Topic areas include:

*   *goal setting*
*   *planning your move*
*   *making the move*
*   *how to set a budget*
*   *developing credit*
*   *staying out of debt*
*   *finding the right apartment*
*   *furnishing the new apartment*

> ** meeting new people / friends*
> ** time management*
> ** legal considerations*
> ** getting / dealing with roommates*
>
> *and much more!*

This book contains several ideas and the plans for accomplishing all of the above, as well as amusing anecdotes and stories that will illustrate the art of living on your own.

CHAPTER 1:

YOUNG REBELS *(With Or Without A Cause)*

You look forward to the day when you can move away from home and live in your own place, probably an apartment at first. It provides you the chance to set up a household and do things your own way. It is the first step in the American Dream. Unfortunately, you could find yourself moving back in with your parents when you are unable to make ends meet. The problem is a lack of preparation. Knowing what you want, and how to get it, is an essential skill you need to master before you move out.

Do You Really Want To Move Out?

(What? Is this guy crazy? Of course I want to move out. That's why I am reading this book.)

I heard that thought, and no I am not crazy (a little bizarre maybe). I ask the question "Do you really want to move out?" because I wonder how much thought you have actually given to making this a reality in your life. I can remember my sister complaining and yelling things at my parents like "I can't wait until I move out and get my own place!" Later on when touring prospective apartments she also made brilliant comments like "You mean I have to pay for the electricity?" Clearly rocket scientist material.

1

Seriously though, we all reach a point where we need our own space. A space without bossy brothers, nosy parents, and sisters always in the bathroom. A place we can call our own to live and grow in the manner of our own choosing. Making the decision at times can seem quite simple, "Okay, that's it! I am not putting up with this situation any longer, I am out of here!" Sometimes family life can drive you over the edge, but it has its good times too.

The Ties That Bind You

Once you move out the connections you have with people, places, and things will no longer exist, at least not in the same way. The neighborhood store with the friendly grocer who knows your name may be out of your day-to-day reach once established in your new home. Household dramas that used to drive you crazy happen now without you. You can call to find out the news but it isn't the same as being there.

Like the time I left out a half gallon of frozen chocolate yogurt and the dog ate it. Later that day the dogs' bowels cut loose all over the place. The poor dog, knowing that restraint of bodily functions was required while in the house, fled the scene in terror, not to return until hours later. I nearly choked to death from laughing as I watched my sister scoop up the mess with paper plates. Of course, I didn't admit leaving out the yogurt until months later.

It will not be easy to share time with friends and acquaintances. Old friends will develop new relationships and become involved in different activities to fill the void your departure creates. The pattern of your life will be forever changed. The saying: "You can never go home" is true. When I go home to visit it seems the dog is the only one who remembers me. (She still lets out a yelp of fright and bolts from the room when I get the yogurt out of the freezer.)

If you move to another part of the country, there may be extreme differences in the climate, local geography, and customs of the people. Each of these differences may require a significant adjustment in your attitude or lifestyle. Basically, what all this amounts to is *change.* One of the most uncomfortable aspects of the human condition, yet the only constant in our lives. Change for many people is the big *"What if ..."* and then fill in all the dire consequences that could happen. Most of these dark imaginings never come to pass.

When I Grow Up I Want To Be ...

... supreme ruler of space, time, and all creation - or the next captain of the starship Enterprise.

One big change when you move out is that now **you will have to work, not choose to work.** While living at home you had the freedom to take a part-time job to make money to buy clothes, pay car insurance, or go out on a date. Now that you want to move out, the big decisions will be "What kind of job do I need to pay my expenses so I can enjoy life on my own?"

Give careful consideration to what kind of job you take. Many people take the first job they get out of high school or college and keep it as though it will be a career. If you are lucky, you may have stumbled upon the very job you want. The chance is better that you should do some research to find a job that you will:

1. Enjoy

2. Receive adequate compensation and benefits.

3. Be able to progress to higher levels of responsibility as well as increased compensation merited by your performance.

4. Have a reasonable amount of security in knowing how

long you will be employed.

5. Be able to achieve specific desires you feel need to be met for the job to be worthwhile.

If you have absolutely no idea what kind of job you would like, or how to go about getting one I suggest you get a copy of the book *"What Color Is Your Parachute?" by Richard Bolles.* It contains all the information you need to know about interviewing, creating a resume, and deciding what career might be best for you.

The Good, The Bad, And The Ugly

I have given you several topics to consider to answer my earlier question *"Do you really want to move out?"* To keep everything in perspective, take a piece of paper and write down all the reasons for moving into your own place. On the other side of the paper, write down all the reasons for staying where you are.

Now that you have all your thoughts down on paper, instead of bouncing around inside your head, it should be easier for you to make your decision. This decision is one of the biggies that you are going to make in your life. If you are not ready, it is a good idea for you to acquaint yourself with the material in this book. It will prepare you for the day you do decide to move. If, however, the quantity or value you place on each reason is sufficiently weighted toward moving out, get ready for some serious planning.

CHAPTER 2:

GETTING YOUR DUCKS IN A ROW
(Goal Achievement Skills)

Your goal? To move out of your current residence and set yourself up in a place you can call your own, a place where you can be king (or queen) of the castle and do as you please. Believe me, once you get the hang of living on your own, you will not willingly live under anyone else's rules again.

The first thing to do is "get all your ducks in a row," or in other words, line up your goals and prepare the plans for the achievement of each. Day in and day out, we act based on our currently dominant thoughts (or goals of the moment). A basic goal, like taking care of an annoying itch, is accomplished by the action of scratching.

ACTION is the key word.

The ability to take consistent action toward your goals and desires while responding appropriately to the feedback produced by such actions is the key to your success. You must be willing to take consistent action toward the goal you have established - moving out on your own. That does not mean once in a while you do something. Taking action means every single day you do something that moves you toward your goal, no matter how small that action

5

may be. It also means that you will do whatever it takes to reach that goal, staying within the bounds of legal, ethical, and moral actions.

What Do You Want?

You must answer this question in detail regarding any goal you may have. The more specific you are the greater your chance of achieving exactly what you want. For the purpose of this book you must decide on such things as:

> *Where do you want to live?*

> *What kind of job do you want (or need)?*

> *What kind of apartment suits your needs?*

> *How much money will you need?*

There are many other considerations outlined within the following chapters that will help you define exactly what you want for yourself when you move out.

Each new goal interacts with every other goal you have. Pretend that all the facets of your life (career, finances, relationships, family, hobbies) are all part of a mobile, like the one that used to hang over your crib when you were an infant. Tugging on any part sets the whole mobile into motion. Each goal, big or small, will affect every goal you have, including your goal to move out. Keep this in mind when making your plans.

The Importance Of Goals

According to author Anthony Robbins you have the choice of *"Making a living, or designing your life."* By setting goals and creating a plan for achieving them you will be designing the life of your choice. Like an archer, you must first have a target (goal) to shoot at before you can hit the bullseye.

Just Do It!

The first step, write out your goals for moving out and setting up your own place. Do it now! Some areas that may interact with your goal to move out might include:

your career

continuing education

financial plans

physical health

personal relationships

family

hobbies

It does not matter what the goals are, just that you write them down, so you can see how they interact with your goal to move out.

How To Achieve All Your Goals

1) **DEFINE** exactly what your goal is, specifically, and in great detail.

Bad Example: I want more money. (Great, if I gave you a dollar you would have more money. Be more specific.)

Good Example: I make $2000 a month.

2) TAKE ACTION to achieve your goal. Do something, anything, that will begin to make this goal a reality. Beginning is the hardest part in achieving a goal. Most of us put things off until a later date. Do something to achieve your goal now. Beginning is half the battle in achieving your goal. Remember the old proverb *"A journey of a thousand miles begins with the first step."*

The first action you can take toward your goal is to **ASK QUESTIONS.**

A. Ask the people, or organizations most associated with your goal, for more information on how to go about achieving what you want. Develop a mentor/student relationship with influential people in the area of your goal.

For example, if I wanted to learn more about living on my own, I would talk to people I felt were living in a manner close to how I would like to live. In addition, I would contact real estate agents, moving companies, and chambers of commerce where I would like to live.

B. Ask for information at libraries, bookstores, computer networks, and universities.

C. Ask any person who can make your goal a reality if they will. The key here is to ask with confident self assurance that what you ask for will be granted. Notice I am not saying that you should become an annoyance or whine to get what you want.

Maybe a relative who lives in an area you would like to move to will let you move in. Placing an ad in a paper you might find a group of people who would like to share rent on an apartment. Someone might be willing to rent a one bedroom apartment in return for yard work or simply providing security for their house while they are away. The possibilities are endless, but you will never encounter them unless you ask. Your very suggestion could provide a solution for someone else's goals.

3) Follow Through. Do something, anything, no matter how small each day towards the achievement of your goal.

4) Network. Spread the knowledge of what you want to as many people as you can. Each contact, or someone they know, just might be in a position to help you.

5) Act "As If." Act as if you have already achieved your goal. Visualize in words, pictures, and emotions exactly what it feels like to achieve your goal. Then behave "as if" the goal is already an accomplishment in your life.

6) Accept Feedback. Use new information to adjust your strategy to achieve your goal. To succeed in any endeavor you must have experience. To get experience you must be willing to make mistakes. Each mistake is feedback on your road to the accomplishment of your goal.

If your goal is to see a sunrise, and you are facing west, you need to change your strategy. Study the feedback from each attempt toward your goal. Determine whether it is in your best interests to continue with the same strategy or adapt and change to reach your goal.

7) Do Whatever It Takes! Staying within the laws of our society, and within the boundaries of your conscience, do whatever it takes to achieve your goal. If you have to wake an hour earlier to visit one more apartment complex each day, do it! No matter what you have to do to achieve your goal of moving out, follow through and do it.

Summary

1. Define exactly what your goal is.

2. Take action. Begin achieving your goal by asking questions.

3. Follow through. Take some action every day toward the achievement of your goal.

4. Network with other people who can help you achieve your goal.

5. Act as if you have already achieved your goal.

6. Accept feedback from all sources to help you adjust your strategy to achieve your goal.

7. Do whatever it takes!

> # *"Do Whatever It Takes!"*

CHAPTER 3:

CHOOSING AN APARTMENT

Where you decide to live, among other factors, will determine your "quality of life" when you move out. Your personal goals and desires will determine which areas of your life take precedence in making this choice. I will, however, touch on key areas that you should consider before renting an apartment.

Where Do You Want To Live?

The main focus of this question is to determine where, physically, you would like to live. Do you wish to remain in the town you grew up in? Would you like to move to another city, state, or country?

Obviously, if you are moving out for the first time, you may not wish to make a move that separates you from many of the resources you have developed and acquaintances you have made in your home town. A job relocation or going to school in another part of the country may cause you to reconsider. Possibly, you may want to strike out on your own and make your first move an adventure.

Forget about where you live right now and fantasize for a moment. If you could choose anywhere in the world to live, where

11

would that be? Based on your current circumstances (or in spite of them) is it possible for you to live there? Think about it for a moment. Would you like to live near a sunny beach? Maybe, you prefer a colder climate in the mountains? A desert region? Living on a tropical island might be nice. Anywhere but Cleveland! (Sorry, Arsenio.)

How will your choice of physical location affect your:

A) career goals

B) future plans

C) finances

D) hobbies

How long would you like to live in this particular area? Is there a significant other? How will that persons' decisions affect where you live?

Uptown, Downtown, Or Out Of Town?

Okay, you have decided, geographically, where you want to live. Now, where would you like to live in relation to the rest of the population? Some people love to be around others so the city is the best choice. The wide open space of the country setting has its charm. For those in between, the comfortable suburbs offer a little of both. Which area would you prefer?

Some considerations in determining the answer to this question may be:

1. How close to public transportation do you need to be?

2. How much of a commute will it be to your place of work?

3. What is your access to major shopping areas?

4. How will your choice of locale affect your financial picture? (Is the rent lower outside of town? Can your car stand the wear and tear of constant commuting? Is the car gas efficient? How much are tolls and parking?)

5. Where are schools and churches located?

6. How accessible are hospitals, medical centers, and daycare?

7. Is the neighborhood improving or decaying?

8. What are the plans for construction and building in this area?

9. How large is the police force?

10. Is the population predominantly one ethnic group? Does it matter?

11. What is the city and state tax?

12. Are there any restrictions or licenses necessary for your type of business in this community?

How To Get The Information

Obviously, this is a lot of information, however, it is easy to track down. Some of the ways you can find out this information are to:

1. Contact the Chamber of Commerce of the town you want to move to and ask them to send you brochures describing the town, its historical background, information about sights, living conditions, future planning, demographics, job market, yearly climate, and any other information you may need.

2. Contact real estate agents for background information on housing and rental costs, as well as personal opinions on the area.

3. Many apartment and home rental guides will send you information about housing and local information. (Check for the *"Apartment Guide"* next to your newsstand, or send for a guide for the area you are interested in.)

4. Libraries carry general information about most areas of the country. Check for the book *"Places Rated Almanac"* for information about where you want to move.

5. Call the information operator and ask for the phone number of local newspapers. Call the paper and have the circulation department send you a copy. The paper will help you get a feel for what the area is like. A copy of the local phone book can also provide you with valuable information.

6. If possible, take a trip to the area and check it out firsthand before making your final decision.

7. Check the magazine racks at your bookstore. Many major metropolitan areas have magazines devoted solely to the lifestyle of that particular area.

Getting information in each of these areas will help in making your decision.

Apartment or House?

I make the assumption that this is your first move (or the first in a long time) so I am going to stay with the more budget-appropriate apartment lifestyle. Groups of people may find renting a house cheaper, or you may find a house outside of town that has rental rates comparable to apartments in town. If these are viable options for you by all means explore them. I have decided to focus on the apartment style of living because it offers several advantages over buying or renting a house.

1. Apartment rental is usually cheaper than a house rental or mortgage.

2. Rental agreements offer the flexibility, in many cases, of paying on a month-to-month basis or choosing a lease that may last for six months to a year. If you decide to move again, it is easier to make arrangements with the landlord than it would be to sell or rent a house.

3. Apartments come furnished or unfurnished depending on your preference.

4. Some apartment complexes offer amenities like swimming pools, tennis courts, Jacuzzi's, and fitness rooms that are included in the cost of your rent.

5. Many apartment complexes offer security gates and guards to keep you safe and secure.

6. Apartments have maintenance people to repair broken appliances, leaky faucets, or overflowing toilets.

7. You don't have to cut the grass or trim the weeds!

8. Many complexes have social activities that allow you to create new friends and acquaintances.

What Kind Of Apartment Do You Want Or Need?

A studio apartment is usually one large room with a kitchenette, bathroom and meager closet space. Moving into higher price ranges are apartments with one, two, or three bedrooms. The larger the apartment the higher the chance of having more than one bathroom and additional amenities like a backyard or balcony. Size will usually be the major factor affecting the cost of the monthly rent.

Questions you will need to ask yourself:

1. How much living space do I absolutely need to feel comfortable?

2. How many people will there be living in this space? Just you; you and your wife or girlfriend; you, your wife, and your girlfriend (call Oprah, I am sure she would love to hear about it); you and a roommate; you and a pet?

3. How much storage space will you need for all your belongings?

4. How long do you intend to stay? If this is a starter place, you may want to start small and work your way to a larger apartment in the future.

5. Will you need space at home to do office work or school work?

Okay, now you should have a better idea of the size of the apartment you want. It may be, when push comes to shove, the depth of your wallet will decide for you.

Upstairs or Downstairs?

Obviously, there are advantages and disadvantages to having an apartment either upstairs or downstairs. Many times apartments on the bottom floor will rent for less, but you get to hear all the

16

moving around upstairs. An upstairs apartment may offer a great view but you may have to walk several flights of stairs. Taking large items, even groceries, in and out will be more difficult.

One very special note: It is my suggestion that you contact the local fire company and find out how high their rescue ladders will extend. Do not rent any apartment higher than the ladders reach unless you bounce really well.

Bates Apartments *(formerly Bates Motel)*

The information so far has concerned a specific apartment and not considered the overall complex. To determine whether you are moving into a good situation, consider the following points.

1. What do the grounds look like? Are they neatly kept and trimmed, or messy and in disarray?

2. Are the personnel, from the landlord or rental agent to the security guards and grounds people, friendly and courteous? (Anyone named Norman? If so, look for peepholes in the walls and don't plan on too many showers!)

3. What are the people like that currently live at this complex? Does their word of mouth praise the complex or condemn it?

4. Are the dumpsters overflowing with trash?

5. How do the buildings look? Are they clean and neat, or in need of obvious repair?

One good way to determine the financial level of the people living in the complex is to check out the cars parked in front of the apartments.

The White Glove Test

When the landlord or rental agent take you on a tour of the prospective apartment, keep notes on everything for comparison with other apartment complexes. Always make sure you get the exact square footage of each apartment you visit and a copy of the floor plan if one is available. If not, it is a good idea to sketch the floor plan for future reference. Visually inspect every apartment you intend to rent and make notes on the following items.

1. Is the carpeting clean? Any peculiar odors?

2. Are the walls freshly painted with no cracks or paint peeling off?

3. Check all the hardware in the apartment, from doorknobs to windows, faucets, closet doors, medicine chests, and locks to be sure they work properly.

4. Be sure all appliances work appropriately by turning everything on and off.

5. Check the number of electrical outlets in every room and find out what kind of current they can handle.

6. Locate the fuse box and circuit breakers for your apartment and have them explained to you.

7. Check to see if there are lights permanently mounted in every room.

8. Ask when the heater was serviced last and what type of energy it uses (i.e. gas, oil, electric).

9. Check the capacity of the water heater (if you like long hot showers) and how long it takes to recycle.

10. Check the water pressure when running the shower in tandem with the sink in the kitchen or the dishwasher.

11. Check the tiles in the bathroom for clean grouting. Also check to be sure that all the drains and the toilet work properly.

12. Has the tap water been tested and safe for consumption? Ask to see a copy of the results. You may want to buy bottled water for cooking and drinking.

13. Check on services like trash and paper collection.

14. Find out when the utility meters are read. Will you need to be present if the meter is locked in your back yard?

15. If your apartment does not have a door that leads directly to the outside, are emergency and common exits appropriately marked? Does the exit have a "push bar" door for immediate release?

16. Is lighting in the hallways and outside the building sufficient?

17. Are inspection or occupancy permits by the township or county necessary before you move in? (i.e. Fire Marshall, Department of Health and Safety)

18. Is covered parking provided for each apartment? How many spaces?

19. Are there locked and secure storage areas for your belongings outside of your apartment?

20. Are you allowed to have pets? What kind and size limitations are there?

21. Are children allowed in the complex?

22. How many spaces are provided for visitor parking and where are they?

23. Are you allowed to add fixtures to the apartment like hanging plants, pictures, and clocks on the wall? Is it possible to re-paint a particular room?

24. What inspections for pest and insects have been done recently? Does the complex employ an extermination service for such nuisance?

25. Have there been tests for radon and methane gases? What were the results?

26. Do all outside doors and windows have weather stripping and storm windows?

27. Are utility hook ups readily accessible? (i.e. electric, gas, oil, water, phone, cable TV, sewer)

28. What are the hours for special services or recreational areas? (i.e. laundry room, swimming pool, tennis court, etc.)

After visiting several apartment complexes you may develop additional questions that are significant to your own goals and plans. Use this list as a starting point and add to it any additional concerns that are appropriate to your situation.

(See checklist in the back of the book)

"Forget about where you live right now and fantasize for a moment. If you could choose anywhere in the world to live, where would that be?"

CHAPTER 4:

Making The Decision

Choosing where you will live is a big decision that will affect your life day to day. What looked like a great apartment complex could change when you find that the neighborhood bar has lots of rowdies that hang out near your parking area. The key in making your decision is to get as much information up front as possible.

When visiting each apartment make a diagram of the floor plan. Take notes on all the benefits and potential problems with each unit you visit. Visit as many different complexes as possible before deciding where you want to live. Keep records on each.

Take a drive around any apartment complex that interests you. See if there are any businesses or situations that could affect your enjoyment of living in this place (i.e. railroad tracks, a nightclub nearby, a school across the street, a park nearby, or a shopping center). Decide if the impact on your lifestyle is acceptable.

Restrictions

Talk to the landlord and have the apartment lease explained in detail. You may find that certain lease restrictions make an enticing apartment a poor choice for your needs. For example, if you have a cat and the lease says pets are not allowed. You may want to rent for six months only and the minimum lease is for a year. If you are not clear on any details in the lease, have someone you trust look it over and give you some advice.

If you are from out of town, time and budget constraints might make it difficult to see many apartment complexes. Find a complex where you can get a month to month rental arrangement. This may cost you a few dollars more at the outset, but you won't be tied to a year long lease in a location that you find through experience to be undesirable. In a worst case scenario, do not take a lease for longer than six months.

Picking A Winner

Once you have compiled your records from visiting apartment complexes, you will know which to discard and which to consider. If you are lucky, you may have stumbled upon a situation that is exactly to your tastes and no further thought needs to be given to the matter. In most cases, you will have whittled your choices down to two or three different apartments. Now you must consider:

1) Your currently dominant goals for the coming year.

2) The budget you have established for the next year.
(Budget? What budget? Relax that comes later.)

3) Your gut feeling about each location.

Each of the three areas described above should be looked at closely in regard to the decision you make about where to live. If your major life goals are enhanced by living at the location you have chosen, and the cost is well within your budget, and you have a good feeling about the place, then go for it.

Unfortunately, you may have to make some compromise with your goals. Possibly, a change in your budget that can further affect your goals. This is a fact of life, however, you should never ignore your gut feeling. The mind collects tons of peripheral information every waking second. It then processes this information to provide us with insights and clues into situations - what we might call hunches. More often than not, these hunches turn out to be correct, so follow them (although in horse races...).

Applications

Once you choose an apartment, the landlord will require you to fill out an application form and in most cases pay a processing fee. The application form is much like the ones you may have used to get credit in the past. In fact, one of the most important things a landlord wants to know is your ability to pay your rent. If you fill the application out at the landlords office, come prepared with checking account numbers, credit card numbers, "nearest relative" addresses and phone numbers, address and phone number of your employer, and any supporting financial documents.

Often, you will have to pay an application processing fee that is in the range of twenty to thirty dollars. This keeps people from filling out applications all over town and wasting a secretary's time. The fee is also used to run a credit check with a credit reporting agency. When you pay the fee, usually non-refundable, a landlord feels you are committed to renting an apartment in that complex. He will give your application more consideration than people who are just shopping around.

If you have the time, you should only place an application with one complex starting with your first choice. If this complex is your first choice, it may also be the first choice of several other applicants competing with you to get an available apartment. Your good credit at this point will be extremely helpful.

"Sign Right Here On The Dotted Line"

Congratulations (hopefully), your application has been accepted and approved, now you only have to go in to the landlord's office and sign the papers. Before you sign any lease be sure you have followed the checklist below:

1. Make sure that all blank spaces in the rental or lease agreement are filled in. Don't accept comments like "we'll fill that in later," even if they tell you what will go in the spot. With your signature on the bottom line you are liable for whatever they decide to "fill in."

2. Confirm the exact amount of rent due, security deposit if applicable, and what date the rental payment is due each month.

3. When is the rent considered late? Are there any financial penalties?

4. Check on what conditions need to be fulfilled to have your security deposit returned if you decide to move.

5. Make sure you understand all your responsibilities and liabilities as stated in the lease agreement. Check with the local court house to be sure the agreement is within the letter of the law. If you do not understand any portion of the agreement, have the landlord explain it to you before you sign it. If you still feel there is a problem have the agreement checked by someone you trust (like your parents) before signing it.

6. Confirm the actual date you can take occupancy. You may be liable for rent, from the first of the month, even if the old tenants are still in the apartment.

7. Be sure that the apartment has passed any local or town inspections from the fire marshall, health inspectors, and exterminators and that you have a valid occupancy permit. Conditions for occupancy may vary from town to town.

8. If you move into a multi-storied structure, you need to reserve the elevator for the day you move in. You also need to get the keys to your apartment.

9. Check on what services come with the apartment and which you will need to pay. You may need to make a deposit with the gas and electric company, phone company, and possibly sewer and trash services.

10. If a service is included in the rent, make sure of your ability to regulate it in your apartment. For instance, some apartments come with heat. Who regulates the temperature, you or the landlord? With any service provided by the landlord check your ability to regulate its effect in your apartment (i.e. cable TV provided by the landlord may have a fuzzy picture because the signal is diffused by so many apartments receiving the signal).

11. Check on the location of your mail delivery. In addition, check on the location and hours of operation of the laundry rooms, recreation centers, and any other amenities offered at the complex.

12. Check on procedures for security systems in your building or complex. How do you contact security in case of an emergency? Are their patrols twenty - four hours a day or only in the evening? Do the gates get locked at night? How do you prove you are a resident? What procedure must friends go through to visit you?

13. What are the policies regarding visitors? May they stay overnight? What if they want to visit for a month? Can you rent out your extra bedroom if you want to? What about pets?

14. What kind of insurance policies cover the premises? Will you need to add a liability policy to your renter's insurance? In most cases, you will be responsible for any damage to the apartment including fire, vandalism, and acts of God. Talk with your insurance agent about renter's insurance to cover your personal belongings and add a liability policy to cover the apartment on the chance of lightning bolts from a divine source.

Avoid future hassles and upset by checking with your landlord about any of your concerns in each of these areas. Once you are satisfied that everything is in order you can sign the lease and prepare to move in.

(See sample "Rental Lease Agreement" on pages 130 and 131.)

CHAPTER 5:

Developing Credit

Before moving out you will want to establish good credit. Landlords, utility companies, and many other businesses will look at your credit history before they deal with you to determine whether you are a good risk. If your credit is bad, it is still possible to do business, however, you may be required to place large security deposits or pay a higher rate of interest for any credit you receive.

To establish a credit history you will need to take out a loan or get a credit card and establish a good paying record. Unfortunately, you can't get a loan or credit card without already having good credit. Catch 22!

The situation is not as hopeless as it sounds, however, you need to make definite plans to establish good credit well in advance of when you plan to move out. The best time to start is now.

Open A Checking Account

An excellent way to develop a sound financial history is to start by opening a checking account at a bank near you. Once you open a checking account you need to keep it in good order with appropriately reconciled statements. That means recording in your check ledger all checks paid and outstanding and keeping track of your balance. If you can do this, and never bounce checks, you will demonstrate to the bank that you are financially responsible.

Open a checking account as soon as possible. This will give you a track record to demonstrate your financial responsibility before you actually need the credit.

Taking Out Your First Loan

An excellent way to develop a good credit history is to take out a loan and pay it back on time. The best time to get a loan is when you don't need it. When you do, it will be extremely difficult to get. Ask anyone who applied for a loan when it was needed. When you buy your first car, you might consider financing it through a bank even if you have the money to pay for the car outright. That way you can begin to develop a good credit history.

The main items that most banks look at when determining whether to give a loan are:

1) job stability,

2) financial responsibility, and

3) length of residence in the area.

Job stability means that you maintain consistent employment within your particular field. A bank usually wants to see that you have maintained a job for at least two years. Moving upward in your job, or even changing to different companies, may not affect you if you show consistent employment within a particular field of work. For example, you start working as a grill cook at McDonald's and then accept a position at a high price restaurant. Your job is still in the food service industry.

The length of residence is how long you have lived in a particular location. Obviously, you may move around your town or state, however, if you move from town to town, or state to state frequently a bank may be uncomfortable giving you a loan. If you do make a move, the credit history developed at your former residence will be looked at closely to determine what credit will be extended to you in your new home.

Financial responsibility is demonstrated by keeping a checking account with all transactions clearly marked and a running balance that coincides with current bank statements. In addition, if you have any other credit accounts with department stores, gas cards, or any business where you have had to make payments on a scheduled basis, the bank will look at these to determine if you have met those obligations in a timely manner.

Armed with financial responsibility, job stability, and length of residence, the bank will probably still turn you down when you apply for your first loan. Remember, banks are primarily in the business of making money. Banks do not want to lose money in risky investments like making loans to people with little or no history of good credit.

What To Do

You may think the information above was a total waste of time that could have been used watching Star Trek reruns, or eating a half gallon of chocolate ice cream, but bear with me.

Once you have developed the credit traits listed above they will be on the positive side of the ledger from the bank's viewpoint. You must remember, the bank has a responsibility to its stockholders and clients to make loans only to people who can pay the loan back on time.

Get A Co-Signer

Ask one of your relatives, preferably one of your parents, if they are willing to co-sign with you on a loan. On the strength of your parents good credit, the bank will give you a loan and allow you to start developing a sound credit history. Remember, however, that both your credit and your parents will be affected if you, for one reason or another, default on this loan.

After you have repaid this loan, go back and apply for a loan in your name only, and again pay it off on time. This will create for you an excellent credit history. I used the loan my parents co-signed for me to buy my first car. By the time I paid off the loan (it was for two years) I was ready to get a nicer car. This time I got the loan by myself and was soon the proud owner of a new vehicle.

Using Your Own Money As Collateral

Another method to develop credit is to put up some form of collateral. Collateral is anything of value that the bank can hold as payment if you do not pay back your loan. Take money you already have in an account and turn it over to the bank as collateral. The bank will keep this money secure (and it will still earn interest) while you make your monthly payment and pay off the loan. Once the loan is paid the bank will release the money kept as collateral back into your possession.

Unless the money you borrow is used for a specific goal, put it into another interest bearing savings account. Pay off the loan with this money. The interest you earn on this money will cut down the amount of interest you pay on the loan. It also will keep you from spending the money on something you may not really want or need.

Incidentally, paying off the loan early may not help you develop the credit you seek. The bank wants to know if you can meet your obligations over an extended period, and that you make your payments promptly.

I Don't Need Credit

Many young people feel they do not need good credit. That may be true, but good credit will make buying a car, renting an apartment, getting gas or credit cards, obtaining medical care, or renting a car much easier and will probably be cheaper. Financial institutions charge those with poor credit higher interest rates to offset the chance that the person may default on the loan. Many of the services you need, like the phone or electric company, may demand hefty deposits if you have poor or no credit. Landlords will almost certainly ask for an additional months rent in advance as well as a security deposit.

Developing good credit may help you keep more money in your account earning interest for you rather than someone else. If you have a problem dealing with money or understanding credit and how to develop it, run, don't walk to your nearest bank. Talk with one of the bank representatives who will tell you what you need to know.

Additional Services

While at your bank also check into "check guarantee cards" which allow you to cash checks with local merchants. Some banks will not issue these cards until the account is active for more than one year. In addition, check into "ATM" cards (Automatic Teller Machines) for when you need cash in a hurry and the bank is closed.

Warning: Getting an ATM card is not a good idea unless you follow through and record all your withdrawals. It is easy to take $20 here and $40 there and forget to record the withdrawals in your check book. In addition, some banks charge as high as $3.50 per ATM transaction. Unfortunately, the reminder of these withdrawals may come in the form of $25 dollar bounced check charges you have to pay when you can least afford it.

A House Of Cards

I have made passing reference to credit cards several times throughout this section. I debated whether it was a good idea to talk about getting credit cards at this point in your life. The conclusion I came up with is that there is nothing inherently wrong with credit cards as long as the user is responsible. Just as guns don't kill people, credit cards do not put people into debt. It is the misuse or lack of responsibility with each that causes problems.

The Sermon On The Mount

Credit cards can create a temptation to spend money that you have not yet earned. That's what credit is, money extended to you on the promise of future payment. In this society, where many feel it necessary to wear only the current fashions, drive a new car, and jet set with the rich and famous, credit cards present a way for the average person to rub elbows with the high rollers. If the base of your financial life is literally a "house of cards," any ill wind fate blows your way will cause your finances to crumble.

Okay, I know it is time to get off my soapbox. After all, I believe the scriptural quote goes something like "let the man without sin cast the first stone." Well, I have an endless number of sins regarding credit cards. I just want to pass on some advice from someone who knows what it is like to overuse credit cards.

Salvation

Now that we are aware of the evils credit cards can pose let's look at the good they can offer. When you are far from home and your car breaks down, having a credit card is a godsend (Praise the lord!). Run out of gas with no cash in your pockets? Need emergency medical treatment? On vacation and all of your money is stolen? Hallelujah, there is always the credit card to save you. (I think I'm becoming a born again charger.)

The Facts of Life

Credit cards are good for tracking your purchases, as long as you pay off the balance each month, and they may cover your purchase with additional warranty or loss insurance. If you do decide to get a credit card for emergencies, or simply convenience, you should be aware of a few facts of life about the use of your cards.

1) When making a purchase never allow the card out of your sight. A card taken into another room can be used to make imprints on several credit slips that are filled out (for any amount) long after you are gone.

2) Never give out your credit card number over the phone. Once anyone knows your card number and date of expiration they can order anything from anybody and charge it to you.

3) Always ask for the carbon slips (if there are any) and immediately tear them up. The carbons contain all the information that is on your card. Anyone going through a dumpster behind the store could find the carbons in the trash and have immediate access to your account.

4) Be sure that all the spaces on the credit slip are filled in. At restaurants, fill in the amount you choose to tip, don't let the waiter do it. Cross out any spaces on the credit slip that are not applicable to your purchase. Blank spaces could be filled in later with "additional charges" that you are not aware of until you get your monthly statement.

5) You may wish to get credit insurance. Many credit card companies offer this at an additional percentage rate each month. This insurance may cover unauthorized use of your card. It also may cover your payments if you are out of work for an extended period. Check with the individual companies for what they specifically offer.

6) If your card is lost or stolen report it to the credit card company immediately. You could be liable to pay for anything that is charged to your card, even if the card was stolen.

If you decide to get a credit card, you only need one of the biggies like *MasterCard, Visa, American Express, or Discover.* Most of these cards are accepted around the world at supermarkets, gas stations, fast food places, and many other locations. Each of these cards may have a yearly fee on top of the percentage they charge each month to lend you the money. Shop around to find the best rate you can on monthly interest charges. Check the financial sections of leading newspapers that list the banks offering cards at the lowest rates.

To get a credit card you will need to fill out credit applications very much like the ones you used to get a loan. Credit companies look for virtually the same information. You may not be able to get a major credit card right away. In that case, you can apply for a gas card or local department store card. Once you have established credit in this manner you can re-apply for a major credit card with a much better chance of receiving one. Once you have received a major credit card, get rid of the rest so you won't be tempted to use each card to its limit and get yourself into debt way over your head.

"Just as guns don't kill people, credit cards do not put people into debt. It is the misuse or lack of responsibility with each that causes problems."

CHAPTER 6:

I can hear several of you complaining, "Oh man, I don't want to read about budgets." I hear you. I hate reading this kind of stuff myself; but it is necessary. I put this section after the more interesting subject of choosing your own apartment on purpose. Unfortunately, if you do not master this section of the book, the reality of living on your own may be a very brief experience. I made this section easy to digest so go ahead and finish it. No dessert until you are done!

Preparing Your Budget

Moving out is an exciting experience. Imagine all the great things you can do with your new found freedom and the luxury of your own place. Achieving that dream can also harness you to some unpleasant realities. You can't stay on the phone all night with your friends because your phone bill will be larger than the national debt. You won't leave the lights on all day, nor will you leave the heater burning after you receive your first utility bill. Many things you took for granted at home will now take center stage in your attention because they cost you *money.*

The best, yet most painful lessons learned are those that cost you money. Money you don't have to throw away because of thoughtless actions. Once you have blown some major bucks you will never make the same mistake again.

Your ability to prepare a budget and stick to it is a major factor in whether you enjoy life once you move out. When you follow your budget you will be working to live the good life. When you don't follow your budget you will be living only to work so you can pay your debts. Budgets equal self discipline.

No budget will be effective until you have determined what your goals are and what lifestyle you plan to live. Before going any further outline your goals. *(See goal information in appendix)*

Some easy parts in establishing a budget are knowing the costs of your rent, food, and car payment. But, how will you fund your goals and aspirations? For example, what if you plan to become a writer? Where you will you come up with the money to get a typewriter or computer, or to take creative writing classes at a local college? Many of your goals and dreams have a monetary cost associated with them that needs to be considered when you make up your budget.

In addition, any major lifestyle changes will have a significant impact on your budget. Getting married will cause a temporary drain on your finances. Farther down the road your marriage may help to build up cash reserves with two incomes paying the expenses. Getting a divorce could be a crushing blow in legal costs and child support. Having a child will cause an immediate and ongoing change in your budget. Any change in your lifestyle will cause a change in your budget and should be considered.

Daily Spending Record

Do you have any idea how much money you spent today, this past week, this past month? I often start the day with twenty bucks in my wallet and in an hour or so I have less than five dollars left. Where did it all go? To find out I started keeping track of my spending habits for a few weeks. You should do the same for a week or two. See if you can find a pattern to your spending and perhaps notice where you are wasting money.

Buy a little spiral bound notebook and keep it in your pocket. Every time you buy something, no matter how much it costs, write it down. It won't take long before you see where your money is

36

going. Insignificant purchases like chewing gum here, a can of soda there, a bag of chips in the afternoon, a newspaper after work, all add up to a substantial amount of money. Look at your checkbook ledger for the past year as well as credit card statements to get more information on where you spend your money.

Keep a notebook for a week or two. Note where you spend money on a daily basis. Do you really need to spend this money or are you buying items on impulse thinking they cost so little they won't affect your budget? These inexpensive items will add up to a respectable amount of money. In the back of this book is a sheet titled *"Daily Spending Record,"* copy it and list all your purchases for the next two weeks.

Impulse Buying

Just as eating on impulse will ruin any figure, so will impulse buying ruin any budget. Plan your spending so your money will not seem to fall out a hole in your pocket. If necessary, add to your budget a predetermined amount of money that you can spend each week on miscellaneous items. Once you have spent your allotment for the week, do not dip into any other area of your budget.

Impulse buying commonly occurs when you go to the store to pick up a few needed items. While at the store you see items you need, or just decide you want, and end up spending an extra fifteen to twenty dollars. For instance, you stop at the store to pick up some milk. On the way to the dairy aisle you notice your favorite crackers on sale and pick up a box. Then you decide to pick up some onion dip to go with the crackers. On the way to the checkout, you decide a couple of wine coolers wo¹ᵈ be great, and why not pick up a video for the evening? Prett   ⁿ have spent much more than you planned.

Determining Your Budget

Having determined your goals and sper

weeks, you should have a better idea of your monetary needs. On the following page is an example of a yearly budget. Study it to get an idea of how to set up your own. In the back of this book are blank copies of this budget form. Simply copy this form and begin to outline your own budget.

Income and Expenses

Feel free to add or delete categories within your budget. For instance, under the category of "Income" you may have your weekly paycheck, tips may provide additional income, a side job for extra cash, or child support. Whatever you do to bring in money should be included under the heading "Income."

Under "Expenses" list any bills you currently pay. Estimate on a monthly basis everything else you will pay when you move out including: rent/mortgage, electric, gas/oil, phone, cable TV, car payment, car insurance, medical insurance, water/trash bill, personal/commercial loans, credit cards, gas cards, department store cards, food, transportation costs (i.e. gas, tolls, parking, maintenance on car), entertainment, clothing, savings, miscellaneous (child support, etc.).

To get a better idea of how much items like utilities will cost, determine what size apartment you want and talk with friends to see how much they pay. Many utility companies can give you rates for an average apartment in the area you live. Rent should not exceed thirty to forty percent of your take home pay.

Check your current home phone bill to see how much you call others and what the cost is per month. List the foods you like and take a walk through the store with pad and paper and write down the costs for a weeks worth of food. Multiply that cost times four to get your monthly cost. Phone logs and shopping lists are provided at the end of this book to help you determine these costs.

When filling out the yearly budget sheet each of the "Expense" d "Income" categories is multiplied by 12 for each month of the

YEARLY BUDGET

Yearly Income: For the year 1994		
Salary / Tips	24,000	00
Bonuses / Commissions	1,200	00
Outside Sources (Alimony, Royalties, Etc.)	0	00
Interest Income / Dividends	0	00
Benefits (Social Security / Welfare)	0	00
Total Yearly Income:	25,200	00

Yearly Expenses: For the year 1994		
Rent / Mortgage	5,040	00
Insurance: Automobile	840	00
Health / Medical / Life	840	00
Property	150	00
Utilities: (Gas, Electric, Water, Etc.)	600	00
Telephone	500	00
Food	1,680	00
Transportation -Gas, Tolls, Parking, Repair	360	00
Installment Loans: Automobile	3,300	00
Furniture	300	00
Other	1,000	00
Credit Cards	2,040	00
Savings	2,500	00
Taxes	4,680	00
School / Continuing Education	400	00
Hobbies / Entertainment	500	00
Miscellaneous (Birthdays, Holidays, Etc.)	300	00
Total Yearly Expenses:	25,030	00

Budget - Take Two

Okay, so now you have filled out your first budget sheet for the next year. That's right, this was only the first. It is going to take some fine tuning to get your budget in line.

Were you shocked? Did your budget barely meet your projected expenses for the next year or did you have plenty of money left over to spend or save? You may have to adjust your needs and wants so you can afford to live on your own. Perhaps, you will have to live in a one bedroom apartment instead of two, in a complex not as nice. The new car may have to wait because the monthly payments are too high. Hey, nobody said it was all sweetness and light when you go out on your own. At least you now have a better idea of your financial responsibility when living by yourself.

Seasonal Expenses

Seasonal costs are those expenses that come around once a year. They can play a major role in making or breaking your budget. Events like Christmas or any religious holiday, birthdays, anniversaries, Valentines Day, Mother's Day, any time you are expected to give gifts can make a significant impact on your budget. Your gift to Uncle Sam on April 15th can make a big difference.

Other yearly costs can include renewing your drivers license, car registration, car inspection, professional licenses or dues, subscriptions, business seminars, vacations, medical exams, as well as cranking up the heat in the winter, or turning on the air conditioning in the summer. Clothes appropriate to the time of year, climate, or even style of employment can make an impact on your revised budget.

"The best, yet most painful lessons learned are those that cost you money."

Savings / Emergency Fund

Perhaps one of the areas you plan to cut is your personal savings. Don't do it! From each paycheck, or any income you receive, take at least ten percent off the top and put it into a savings account.

ALWAYS PAY YOURSELF FIRST!

Why? Someday you might want a new car. You may need a down payment to get a new home. You may be married and have a child on the way. The chance investment you have been waiting to make in yourself and your career comes along and you need the money to make it a reality. Besides, if you cannot take the responsibility to pay yourself each month, it is doubtful you will follow through with other financial responsibilities.

If those are not enough reasons then do it because you may need an emergency fund to fall back on if you lose your job, or the car mechanic says you need new brakes. With an emergency fund equal to roughly three months expenses you will have a cushion to keep you on your feet in rough times.

Now go back and do your budget one more time.

Cutting Costs

By now, you have a much better idea of what it will cost to live on your own. One of the problems however is that you grew up in a society where you want the good life you saw on television and you want it now. That is not a realistic way to expect life to treat you, however, you can learn to enjoy the benefits of living in a country such as ours.

Some ways to enjoy the benefits offered to the public are:

1) Check the newspaper for free plays or concerts in the park as well as many other community sponsored activities.

2) Tape television shows with your VCR instead of investing in cable television. There are tons of good television shows each week. You cannot possibly have the time to watch every show everyday. You can, however, store them on video tape to watch later. Ask friends who have cable to tape movies or specials for you. Trade video tapes with friends to see current movies.

3) Go to the public library and borrow books, videos, music cassettes, and sometimes even pieces of art.

4) Although phone companies tell us to *"reach out and touch someone,"* you can do it by way of a first - class letter rather than long distance telephone rates. Most people love to get personal letters.

5) Rent videos instead of going to the movies.

6) Keep your heating and air conditioning bills lower by wearing warm sweaters or snuggling with a friend in the winter and using a fan in the summer.

7) Buy larger economy size portions of food at the store and cook and freeze them for future use. Larger portions cost less and cooking all at once uses less energy. Meal size portions can be re-heated with less energy.

8) Ride your bike, carpool, or use public transportation to cut down on the wear and tear to your car and to lower fuel and maintenance costs. Fewer miles per week on your vehicle also could lower your insurance rates.

9) Pay off your credit cards every month. Do not allow the balance to grow or you may soon be only servicing your debt (i.e.

covering the interest charge without lowering the amount you owe as principal). Debt bondage is the modern form of slavery in our society. Once you have stretched your credit to the point that you are just meeting the monthly minimum payment you will begin to feel the squeeze from your creditor's handcuffs as they take away your financial freedom.

Review Your Budget

This chapter is probably the most difficult. Many people spend more time planning a vacation, or a party, than they do designing their lives. If you make the mistake of failing to plan (create a budget), then you are planning to fail. Be on purpose. Know why you are spending your money. Do so to achieve your goals and aspirations and enjoy a happy and successful life.

This should be the first of many times you plan a budget. Every quarter to half of a year review your budget. Determine if changes are necessary to keep you on track with your goals.

"Just as eating on impulse will ruin any figure, so will impulse buying ruin any budget."

CHAPTER 7:

Paying Your Bills

Assuming you followed the directions in this text, you should now have established your budget for the year, or at least for the next six month period. Hopefully, you are ending each month with a positive balance (money left over) or at worst a zero balance (income and expenses were exactly equal) with no money left over after meeting the budget. If you had a negative balance, stop right here. Whittle down some luxuries and items you can do without for a while until your cash flow shows your can meet monthly expenses.

Once you have established a budget you are comfortable with, you need to determine the payment schedule for your bills.

Paying Your Bills On Time

Your budget shows the payments you have to make monthly, but does not indicate when they are due. Creating an appropriate payment schedule is necessary to keep you from replaying the feast and famine routine throughout the month and year.

When you pay your bills is determined by how often you get paid. Some people are paid weekly, others every other week, and some people get paid monthly. Each of these schedules has factors that will affect your spending and bill paying styles.

People who get paid weekly sometimes use a couple extra

dollars from that week's paycheck on some item they absolutely must have, reasoning that next week they will pay the bill they put off this week. Similarly, people who get paid twice a month have a larger amount of money and sometimes spend the excess instead of applying it toward bills from the second half of the month. Not only will this game slowly waste your money, at some point (probably less than a year) you will owe much more than you have. At that point your creditors will start knocking at your door.

Monthly Payment Schedule

The solution is to create a monthly payment schedule. Grab any current calendar and mark down when your bills are due. Take each of your bills or statements and look where it says "due date." That is the time of the month the payment is due. Most statements also include a date after which you owe additional interest or a late fee. Using the calendar list under the appropriate date when each bill is due. When you are done, look at the calendar to see if all your payments occur at one particular time of the month. Rent is usually due within the first few days of the new month. Most other payments can be moved to accommodate the schedule on which you receive your salary.

For example, if you get paid weekly, the last check from the previous month will probably go toward paying your next months rent with a little money left over for some groceries. You will then want to schedule other "major" payments to coincide on a weekly basis with subsequent paychecks. Remember, the money left over from each weekly check may need to be added to future leftovers to pay bills that come due later in the month. It is this money that you must not spend, thinking you can cover the bills with future paychecks.

Schedule your payments so they are spread out through the month and not coming due all at one time. The feast or famine syndrome occurs when you get all your money at once each month and immediately spend it to pay your bills and maybe buy a few frills. Within a week the money is gone and you end up waiting and praying for the next paycheck.

Based on your pay schedule you may want to call your creditors and rearrange your payment due dates with them. Most creditors are happy to do this if it means that you will consistently pay your bills at this time each month. If you have a spouse or roommate, their pay schedules could affect when you schedule your monthly

At this point you may realize that living on your own is serious business with very few margins for error. When watching the homeless on the street I am constantly reminded of the phrase "There but for the grace of God (and a good budget) go I."

Balancing Your Checkbook

In keeping with that thought, this next section is perhaps quite appropriate. A mistake in balancing your checking account, when you have a very tight budget, can lead to a cascade of problems that could put you out on the street or begging your parents to let you come home.

Important basics to remember about your checking account:

1) Your checkbook will not balance itself.

2) Service charges must be deducted monthly, they will not disappear.

3) ATM withdrawals must be included in your check ledger.

4) The bank will charge you upwards of $20 every time you bounce a check, and so may the merchant who received the check!!

How To Become A Bag Lady Or A Bum

Although facetious, the title of this section may be accurate. Consider that your budget has a margin of error of only $50, which for many people is not an unrealistic amount. You have not kept up to date in balancing your checkbook and as a result you have forgotten to deduct the monthly service charge for this month and last, as well as an ATM withdrawal. All your payments have been sent out to your various creditors. You think life is great. About one week later you get a notice from the bank that you have overdrawn your account. In addition, you are being charged a $25 fee for bouncing a check.

The problem can escalate from here. The merchant may re-deposit the check. If it bounces again, you are going to be charged another twenty - five dollars. If any of these penalties deplete your account enough they could cause other checks to bounce resulting in even more bounced check charges. Add to this the fact that most merchants charge additional fees for bounced checks and your budget may be history.

Solution

Don't bounce checks! Rather obvious, I grant you, and possibly of no help once you have bounced a few checks, but it is still the best solution to the problem.

If you have already bounced a check, call the bank immediately to find out what their version of the story is. It may be a clerical error. Your deposit may not have cleared yet (meaning the funds are unavailable for your use), or your checkbook balance is in error because you have not kept it up to date.

Whatever the reason, contact the merchant in question and ask them to hold the check. Tell the merchant you will come in and pay for the transaction in cash. That will keep the merchant from re-depositing the check and causing you further charges. If additional merchants are affected, call them immediately and ask them to hold your check for a few days until you straighten out your account. They may hold the check to keep from going through the hassle of messing up their own books.

At this point, you need to go over your checkbook and make sure everything is in order. If the error is your fault, the bank and the merchants affected are under no obligation to release you from the penalties you have incurred. Scenes from *"Wayne's World"* come to mind where you might get on the floor and beg forgiveness wailing "I'm not worthy, I'm not worthy!" It could work, and "monkeys might fly out your butt!" as Wayne would say. Seriously, in a "first offense" case the bank may drop the bounced check charge depending on the number of checks bounced, and depending on how polite and courteous you are. If you are a chronic check bouncer, be prepared to pay the penalties. The next thing you should do is ask one of the bank representatives to go over with you how to balance your checkbook.

Keeping Your Finances Straight

When you first open your account, find out from your banker exactly what the charges for the use of your account are. There may be a charge for:

1) the printing of your checks;

2) every check written, or you may only be able to write a specified number per month with no charge;

3) each withdrawal using your ATM card;

4) not maintaining the minimum monthly balance on deposit.

There are many kinds of accounts, each with advantages and disadvantages. I suggest obtaining what are sometimes called the "no frills" account. With this type of account, there is no minimum monthly balance. There may be little or no service charge and usually you will receive no interest on the money you keep in the account. In the beginning, this is the best type of account to have to keep track of your finances.

If you are a full time student, the bank may have a special account which charges no monthly fee. You will need a student I.D. to take advantage of this type of account.

Reconciling Your Bank Statement

With each account, you will receive a check ledger that provides spaces to enter the amount of your deposits and withdrawals (with accompanying blanks for check numbers, date, and name of payee) as well as an area to keep a running balance (the amount of money currently in the account). There is also a "check off" area to place a check mark when you confirm the deposit or the payment listed on your statement.

When you receive your monthly statement from the bank you should:

1. "Check off" in your check register all the checks that have been paid according to that monthly statement.

2. "Check off" all deposits credited according to your monthly statement.

3. Add to your register any monthly service charges, ATM withdrawals, or electronic payments. (Sometimes check printing charges.)

"Your checkbook will not balance itself."

Sample Check Ledger:

CHECK #	DATE	DESCRIPTION OF TRANSACTION	PAYMENT		CREDIT		BALANCE	
✓ 0324	3/2	FOX APARTMENTS	450	00			630 00 / 450 00	
✓ 0325	3/3	SUPER MARKET	32	80			180 00 / 32 80	
✓	3/6	ATM WITHDRAWAL	20	00			147 20 / 20 00	
	3/15	DEPOSIT PAYCHECK			770	00	127 20 / 770 00	
	3/17	BANK SERVICE CHARGE	9	00			897 20 / 9 00	
✓ 0326	3/18	PACIFIC POWER CO.	45	73			888 20 / 45 73	

CHECK #	DATE	DESCRIPTION OF TRANSACTION	PAYMENT		CREDIT		BALANCE	
✓ 0327	3/19	ACE AUTO INSURANCE	64	00			842 47 / 64 00	
	3/21	ATM WITHDRAWAL	40	00			778 47 / 40 00	
	3/21	CHECK REORDER CHARGE	12	50			738 47 / 12 50	
0328	3/24	CAR PAYMENT	175	94			725 97 / 175 94	
0329	3/25	CLOTHES STORE	122	56			550 03 / 122 56	
0330	3/25	RECORD STORE	29	33			427 47 / 29 33	

Go over your monthly statement again to make sure you have checked off all deposits, checks paid, service charges, or any other special service fee. At this point you will probably have some checks (or deposits) still outstanding since the bank issued the statement. Add the amount of the outstanding checks together and write it down on a piece of paper under the heading "outstanding checks." Next add the balance as stated on your monthly statement to any deposits not recorded on the statement. This new balance minus the amount of the outstanding checks should equal the balance in your checkbook.

If the balance on your bank statement (after all your figuring) does not equal the balance in your checkbook you may need to check that your mathematics are correct, not only in figuring your monthly statement but also in your adding and subtracting within your checkbook ledger. Be sure all deposits and withdrawals are accurately recorded. Check to make sure you have included all monthly service charges and withdrawals from ATM's.

In addition, make sure you have reconciled any previous bank statements correctly. After reviewing your account, if there is still a problem you should make an appointment to see a bank representative to straighten it out.

ATM's and Electronic Transfers

Right now, when you are first out on your own, I am going to suggest that you may not want to use such bank services as the ATM (Automatic Teller Machine) or Electronic Transfers. While the ATM is great in its versatility and in its ability to let you use the bank twenty - four hours a day, there are some hazards. One, you may forget to record an ATM withdrawal while you are out late partying or impressing your date. Forgotten entries can lead to bounced checks, and since we have been through that scenario you know where that can lead. In addition, deposits made at ATM's generally take longer to process than those done directly at the teller window. That may cause some problems if you thought your money was available for use.

If you do use an ATM, my suggestion is to have it connected to a special savings account and not connected with your checking account to reduce the chance of accidentally overdrawing your checking account.

SPECIAL WARNING: Keep yourself alert and aware when using an ATM machine, especially at night. Muggers and other unsavory individuals may stake out a cash machine. Once you have cash in hand they will be happy to relieve you of the burden of spending it all on your own.

Electronic Fund Transfers

I definitely dislike the idea of Electronic Fund Transfers. Personally, I don't like the idea of someone being able to use my account at will. Second, although bankers claim few problems, I have heard of several cases where multiple withdrawals were made for the same payment leaving the account empty and causing additional problems for the bank customer. Finally, be sure you actually have the cash in the account on the day the transfer is made or you will receive what amounts to a bounced check charge from whatever merchant was unable to withdraw the funds. When you are starting out it may be better for only you to have control over your bank account. Besides making out your checks monthly will help you stay in tune with your budget at the outset when it is most important.

> **"There but for the grace of God (and a good budget) go I."**

CHAPTER 8:

Nickels And Dimes

One of the advantages of living at home is that all the basic supplies for many household activities have been provided for by your parents. A glass breaks you automatically go to the closet and get the dustpan and broom to clean it up. Do you have a dustpan and broom? The dishes are dirty and you go to wash them; did you remember to get dish washing soap? You decide to make yourself an omelet and then realize you have nothing to grease the frying pan with, or worse, you go to use the bathroom and realize you forgot to buy... I think you see what I mean!

Once you move in and set up each of the rooms in your house or apartment (I am assuming at least a kitchen, bathroom, bedroom, and a living room) you will notice that besides the big ticket items like your bed, or pots and pans in the kitchen there are several other necessary items the cost of which will nickel and dime you to death.

For instance, the basic condiments that you might need in the kitchen: salt, pepper, sugar, mustard, mayonnaise, butter, ketchup, as well as paper towels, aluminum foil, plastic wrap, scouring pads, napkins, cooking oil, spices and the list goes on. Each of these represents only a dollar or two in cost but when added together they will increase your shopping bill substantially and more than likely blow your budget.

Make an inventory of all the items you currently have. Many times I have gone to the store to buy something I already had enough of, just when I could have used the money for other things. Keeping a list of the essential basics is good for making out shopping lists. Walking through the store and deciding on impulse that you need or want the item displayed is the worst way to try and stay within a budget. Only buy those items that are on the list you made before you went to the store.

The following lists will outline some of the basics needed for each room in your house:

Kitchen - Major Items
Silverware
Plates / Bowls
Glasses / Cups
Assorted Cooking Utensils
Pots / Pans
Can Opener, Strainer
Baking Pans
Tupperware
Toaster Oven / Toaster (*)
Microwave oven (*)
Blender
Trash Can
Kitchen Table / Chairs (*)
Refrigerator (*)
Grill / Barbecue (*)
Measuring Cups
Napkins
Dish Soap
Dish Towels
Trash Bags
Plastic Wrap
Broom / Dustpan
All purpose cleaner

Basic condiments
Salt / Pepper
Sugar
Spices
Butter / Margarine
Ketchup
Mustard
Mayonnaise
Relish
Coffee or Tea / Creamer
Bread
Cooking Oil
Peanut Butter / Jelly
Syrup
* * * * * * * * * * *
Smoke Detector (*)
Ice cube trays
Paper Towels
Dish Cloth
Pot Holders
Aluminum Foil
Mop / Bucket
Floor cleaner
Scouring pads / Sponge

Add or delete from this list as necessary. (*) means the apartment may already have these items.

Let's move on to the bathroom.

Bathroom - Major Items	**Basic Supplies**
Bath Towels	Toilet Paper
Hand Towels	Tissues
Wash Cloths	Tub / Tile Cleaner
Bath Mat	Shampoo / Conditioner
Shower Curtain (?)	Soap / Skin lotion
Toilet Brush	Deodorant
Razor Blades	Shaving Cream
Tooth Brush	Tooth Paste / Floss
Hair Brush	Hair spray
Nail Clippers	Mouthwash
Weight Scale	Perfume / Cologne
Clothes Hamper	Disinfectant
Trash Can	Toilet Cleaner
Blow Dryer / Curling Iron	Q-Tips
Night Light	Feminine Products

The above does not include such additional items that may be associated with this room such as birth control devices, medicines and medical supplies, cosmetics such as eyeliner, mascara, nail polish and remover, lipstick, foundation, styling gel, and many other products.

Responsible Social Commentary

Remember the commercials about drugs where a guy cracks an egg, drops it into a sizzling frying pan and says "this is your brain on drugs?" Imagine the same kind of commercial for AIDS where a guy is holding the nozzle of a vacuum cleaner hooked to your genitals saying "this is your body with AIDS" and then he switches it on and begins to suck the very life out of your body. AIDS is a horrifying reality, drugs are only a little less scary. Play it safe, don't do drugs, and always protect yourself when you plan to do the "wild thing" with anyone.

This has been a public service announcement brought to you by the author of this book, we now return to the regularly scheduled program.

Living Room - Major Items
Television
Video Recorder / Blank Tapes
Couch / Chairs
Lamp
Cassette / CD Player
Book Case / TV Stand
Curtains / Blinds
Pictures / Posters
Coffee & End Tables
Coat Rack
Magazine Stand

Home "Work" Area
Desk / Table / Chair
Phone
Stationery / Envelopes
Stamps / Phone Log
Computer / Printer
Lamp
Filing System
Return Address Stamp
Phone Book
Calendar / Clock
Appointment Book
Answering Machine

Additional items that may or may not be provided in your new abode: air conditioner, heater, and a fan.

Bedroom - Major Items
Bed /Frame
Sheets
Mattress Protector
Hangers
Clock /Radio / Cassette
Trash Can
Smoke Detector
Pictures / Posters
Jewelry Box

Pillow / Pillow Cases
Blankets / Comforters
Chest of Drawers
Table Lamp
Table / Desk
Curtains / Blinds
Chair
Suit Cases
Mirror

Some items relating to **Laundry:**

Laundry Baskets	Laundry detergent
Drying rack	Fabric Softener
Laundry Bags	Iron
Change for machines	

While you probably have an adequate wardrobe for the time being, review it to make sure it is appropriate for the climate of the place you will live as well as the employment you will have when you are on your own.

Clothing - Basic Necessities

Shoes \ Polish	Pants
Underclothes	Shirts
Jackets	Formal Wear
Raincoats	Sleepwear
Sports Clothes	Skirts / Dresses
Glasses / Contacts	Medical Devices

* Any special clothes appropriate to climate conditions or sports related activities.

Initially, when you move out, you want to keep your out of pocket expenses to a minimum. It is a good idea before you make the big move to have your hair cut and styled, visit the doctor or dentist, generally take care of any situations where you use people you are comfortable with. In your new home, these professionals may be out of reach or too inconvenient to use.

The final list in this section is a shopping list. This list will only portray the most generic items you will want to stock your shelves with initially. It is a good idea to keep a log of your favorite foods and meals before you go shopping.

Food Shopping List

Dairy:	Meats:	Fruits:	
Milk	Chicken	Apples	Pears
Eggs	Beef	Oranges	Cantaloupes
Butter	Fish	Peaches	Pineapples
Ice Cream	Pork	Grapes	Bananas
Cheese	Other	Cherries	Strawberries

Vegetables:	Breakfast Foods:	Miscellaneous:
Corn	Fruit Juices	Pasta
Green Beans	Cereals	Sauces
Carrots	Bagels	Soups
Peas	Pancakes	Rice
Potatoes	Waffles	Noodles
Broccoli	Syrup	Prepared Foods
Cauliflower	Coffee / Tea	Snack Foods
Spinach	Hot Chocolate	Soft Drinks
Lima Beans	Bread	Desserts
Mushrooms	Sausage / Bacon	
Tomatoes		
Lettuce		
Radishes		
Green Peppers		
Cucumbers		

CHAPTER 9:

You Can't Always Get What You Want

When you first set up your household, you may feel that you need all sorts of things to make your place a comfortable home. When you go to the store, you see all sorts of items you believe you actually need; that is not the case. Many people were brought up desiring and getting almost everything they wanted. Their parents were more than willing to provide them what they didn't have as children. The purse strings are tighter today. Anything we want we are going to have to plan for to afford it.

In the previous section, there are lists of items necessary for each room of the house, or are they? What I listed, in reality, are the items we are used to having in each of these rooms. I have had the good fortune to travel and live in other countries. I found that many of the things we take for granted the rest of the world does without. It does not seem to be a hardship for these people.

In the United States, we are used to having three television sets per house, phones in every room (even our cars), microwave ovens, refrigerators with ice makers, and all sorts of devices to make every chore easy. If you plan to have these modern marvels in your household you better get to work on your savings right now. You are going to need quite a bit of cash. If you wait until you move out to get all the items you want you are going to be out a healthy chunk of change that you may not have to spare.

Consider the basic items you need to keep up with the rest of America: a color television set, a CD/Cassette stereo or boom box, a video recorder, a microwave oven, touch tone phone and answering machine. I will stop here although there may be other items that you *absolutely* must have. Even if you bought everything on sale this short list would cost at least a thousand dollars.

Considering that when you first move there are several deposits and payments to get you up and running (i.e. 1st & last months rent, security deposit, electric, gas, phone deposits, and stocking the cupboards initially) that can add up to another $1500 plus or minus a few hundred - we are talking some serious bucks.

The purpose of this section is to get you to start planning the purchase of some of your big ticket items well in advance of your moving out and possibly storing them in anticipation of that day.

How To Get What You Want

ASK.

Actually, the first step is to know what you want. Turn to the section where I listed the items needed for each room and check off those items you currently have. Then go through the list and determine the absolute basics that you still need, like a bed, a chair, kitchen implements. Now that you know what you need, ask for it.

The technique is so simple yet many people never think to try it. When I say ask I do not mean beg, and I certainly do not mean whine. I do mean, clearly and with a positive expectancy that the person will provide you with what you need, ask for the items in question. You will be surprised at the number of people who will help you out when you ask them nicely, and of course, thank them profusely afterward.

Who Can You Ask?

Start with your family members and relatives. Your parents may be happy to let you take the bed you slept on for years. That old couch in the rec room needs to be replaced, so by all means, take it they will say. There are all sorts of items around the house collecting dust from disuse simply because no one knows what to do with them and they are too good to throw out. In this instance, you may actually be doing them a favor helping them to clear out a bunch of clutter. Similarly, friends of the family and relatives living in other locales may have items they want to be rid of that you can use to create a comfortable lifestyle in your new home.

Ask Co-Workers

Place a notice on the bulletin board at work and let co-workers know what items of household furniture or appliances you need. You may get them for free or for a greatly reduced price over the same item new from the store.

Barter

You may run across multiples of certain things. A friend received two toasters as wedding presents and will trade you for an extra electric can opener you have. Ask or you will never know.

Flea Markets

Flea markets are an excellent outlet for purchasing low cost items you may need. Many communities have flea markets where people come to sell all sorts of products. I would not recommend buying the supposedly "new" stereos or televisions. If there is something wrong with them you may have no warranty or guarantee to fall back on. In some cases, these items may be cheap imitations or knock-offs.

Garage Sales

Garage sales offer you an excellent opportunity to get super bargains on all sorts of items. Many people are looking to get rid of little used or unwanted items to cut down on shipping costs when they move and will take most offers.

A few hints when going to a garage sale:

1) Always carry money in a variety of denominations, so you can pay the exact price. If you talk someone down from twenty dollars to twelve dollars, and then give them a twenty hoping for change, you might be out of luck.

2) Always make an offer much lower than you expect to pay. You might get lucky and they will take the offer. At the very least you can work your way to a middle ground that is acceptable to both of you.

3) The early bird catches the worm, or in the case of garage sales, the best deal. If you sleep-in Sunday and go out in the afternoon to all the garage sales you will find that all you get to do is pick through the leftover albums of the Partridge Family.

4) Map out all the sales you want to go to by checking in the newspaper where and when they will be located.

5) Call the people who list the items they have for sale in advance if there is an item you particularly want. They may invite you to come over the night before and give you first choice.

6) Be prepared to transport the item home immediately. Never leave an object you have purchased at a sale while you check elsewhere as your purchase could disappear.

7) As stated earlier, if you don't see an item that you would like ask the person holding the sale about it. There may be some items they initially intended to keep that they may change their mind about and sell to you for a good price. You will never know unless you ask.

Newspaper Ads

If you can't find what you want in any of these areas you may be able to get it through a newspaper ad. Check the classifieds for what you want and see if anyone is offering it for sale. If not, you can place an ad for the very thing you want at very low rates. Some papers are of the trade and barter variety where you can trade something you have for something you want.

Newspapers also carry special coupons for additional discounts. Cutting coupons can keep your costs down when buying food products and supplies for the house. The Sunday newspaper will carry lots of coupons and notices of special sales.

Keep your eyes open when you get your mail. There will be tons of "junk mail," however, now and then you might find specials offered by local business.

Paying the Price

Sometimes the items you want are not going to be found at a garage sale and you will have to buy them at a store. In that case, it may be a good idea to check with all the local stores for the item you want. Calling each store will save you gas and time and give you a good idea who stocks the particular item.

Discount Stores

Before buying the item at any local store check out the discount stores. What I mean are these new mega-stores that sometimes have a membership fee. You can save a lot buying at these outlets. In addition, many factory outlet stores are popping up where you can buy direct from the factory or get items that are used or slightly damaged for a significant discount.

When To Buy

I am really stretching the thrifty theme now but if you can plan your purchases for after major holidays like Christmas, Thanksgiving, and New Years you may be able to get great bargains.

Buy Quality

Regardless of what it is that you are purchasing, do yourself a favor and always buy the best quality that you can afford. In addition, if a warranty is offered - take it. Many items like your TV or VCR you don't want to replace year after year, so buy a quality product that you know the manufacturer will stand behind. No matter how good a deal looks, if the product is inferior and breaks down it may cost you more than the higher priced quality item would have.

If you have no idea what items are of better quality then visit your local library and read the latest edition of **"Consumer Reports"** concerning the product in question. This magazine will give you an idea of costs, maintenance records, and all the variable styles of a particular item.

Now you know how to get all the items you want to set up your new household. When you find a good price on an item you want, purchase it and store it for the day you make your big move. Store each item safely so it neither deteriorates because of the elements or through neglect, and that it is not stolen or misplaced.

CHAPTER 10:

Cleaning Your Closets

When you are ready to move, you must decide exactly what you are going to take with you. You probably have tons of stuff, most of which you have not used in the last decade or may even have forgotten that you owned.

I have traveled all over the USA and a few other countries taking jobs and living in various locales. Each time I moved I packed all my stuff and shipped it ahead of me. I paid a fortune in shipping charges. After one particular move, I noticed some boxes I had shipped to California, Australia, Bermuda, and back to the USA that I had never opened. Obviously, the items were:

A. expensive souvenirs

B. important tax papers

C. sentimental keepsakes

D. my old Playboy collection

E. None of the Above

"E" would be the correct answer in this case. After opening the boxes and throwing out useless or outdated material I had enough stuff left to fill only half of one of the four boxes I had been shipping. Oh, dopey me!

Throughout your life, you have collected an assortment of odds and ends. Looking at your treasures, you probably think, "I don't have any use for this, but it's not junk so I won't throw it out. You never know when I might need it."

The rule of thumb in deciding what to keep and what to get rid of is whether you have used the particular item within the last year. If you have, keep it. If not, donate it to the Salvation Army or some other charitable organization. You may be able to deduct the value of the item from your taxes.

Obviously, there may be items you have not used that are too valuable to give away. Things like computers, TV's, antiques, or sentimental items. Other items may be seasonal like winter clothes, or sports related like ski gear. Decide if these items still fit in with your lifestyle and the lifestyle you can afford when you move.

Eliminate unnecessary items by trading for things you do need with your friends. Maybe, you have an old black and white TV set you don't use that your neighbor can stick in her kitchen and watch while fixing meals. She might trade for the extra toaster she got from her wedding last year.

The purpose for cleaning your closets and eliminating unwanted items is to cut down on the cost of your move. If you happen to be using a professional mover they are going to charge you by the pound for moving your belongings. If you are going to do the moving yourself or with friends it will still cost you extra to move unwanted items by having to rent a larger truck, extra expense for boxes, and the wear and tear on yourself carting the extra baggage. Believe me, after you start going through your stuff, you are going to start eliminating many things when you determine the end cost.

Garage Sale

Help pay for the cost of your move by having a garage sale. Clean off anything that looks good and slap a sticker on it with a suggested price. On the day of the sale, you can have fun dickering with people over the best price you can get. Remember, you are trying to get rid of the stuff so don't push it too far.

A few days in advance of your sale place a notice in the classified section of your newspaper. Clearly state the date, time, and location of your sale. List some of the better items you have for sale to pique the customer's interest. Next, make some signs that say "Garage Sale Today" with your street address and arrows that point the way to your house. Place these signs at intersections near your home so they will attract drive by traffic.

Remember to go to the bank the day before to have some change on hand. Sales could be lost if you are unable to make change. You can hire a big lug named Bruno to guard the money during the sale.

Have your sale set up and ready to go well in advance of the time you have stated. Many thrifty bargain hunters will show at the crack of dawn hoping to get the best bargains. Some may even try to get at your stuff the night before!

Depending on the weather, you can also make a few extra bucks selling sodas and hot dogs on the side (or give away free with every purchase). Many people rush from sale to sale and become hungry and thirsty. The added benefit is that people buy more when you are also helping to satisfy some of their basic needs. After the sale, whatever is left over you can donate to local charities or give to your neighbors. Remember though that any donations may be tax deductible.

If you have any flammable items such as gasoline, or propane in your barbecue you need to use it up or give it away. Transporting flammable items in many areas of the country is not allowed, especially if your route of travel to your new home will take you through tunnels or on toll roads.

Collections And Returns

Now is a good time to go around and visit all your friends who have borrowed things from you in the past and collect them. Everything from jackets, books, CD's, money, whatever they have borrowed from you. If you are only going across town this may be unnecessary, however, if you are moving some distance it is better to get it now than write a letter and get them to send it to you later.

Collect anything you have at the dry cleaners and pick up any layaway purchases. Anything you have on hold at any merchant should be picked up now. If you are expecting packages that may coincide with the time you are moving you may want to call the merchant or person and leave forwarding instructions with them. Be sure to collect any deposits you have made with businesses or services in your area (i.e. deposit for phone, check being held by video rental store, etc.)

Return anything you have borrowed from anyone or any business or organizations. Some of these items might include library books, video tapes, anything you have borrowed from a friend, especially money. If you have borrowed money as a loan for a car, student loan, or anything of that nature notify these people before you leave town if you are unable to pay off the note.

Repair/Replace/Paint

If you have done any damage to your room from hanging posters or punching holes in the wall you should repair or replace the broken items, or paint over any areas that need it. Your parents/landlord may want to remodel the room anyway but it never hurts to offer.

Let's Play Dress Up

Now that you have everything out of your closet you might as well see if it still fits. Remember as a kid when you used to go through all your clothes and play "dress up?" If you had sisters you probably could. At any rate, there may be some pieces of clothing that no longer fit. Instead of paying extra to ship what won't fit, have fun for an afternoon trying everything on and decide what to take with you. Even with closets full of clothes, many people have a certain set of clothes they habitually wear to the exclusion of all else, either because of fashion changes or body changes.

If you have not worn something in over a year, it is a good idea to donate it to the Goodwill or Salvation Army. Keep any item of clothing that may come in useful for the weather conditions at your new home. Also, remember that your budget may be limited for a time so any article of clothing that can be recycled into your wardrobe should be kept.

Take Out The Trash

By this time, your room probably looks like Hurricane Andrew has hit it. Carefully sift through all the rubble and throw out or give away everything you don't need. This will make taking inventory of your belongings a much easier process.

Inventory Your Belongings

All right, now you have eliminated all of the stuff you don't need. You should have cleared out the clutter and only be left with those items you want to take with you. Now you should sit down with a pen and paper and inventory all the items you have. This also will serve to let you know what items you still need to get for your new household. If you are extra lazy and don't feel like writing everything down you can grab a video camera and film all your belongings. The video will provide you a visual record of everything you own. This video record also may be valuable in jogging your memory about what you did with an item when you packed it.

CHAPTER 11:

The Best Way To Move

What is the best way to move to your new household? The answer depends on your particular situation. Here are a few ideas so you can decide for yourself what method is best.

The first consideration is how far away you are going to move. Just across town?, in that case, you can probably take things over to your new apartment a bit at a time. If you make a move to the other end of the state or across country, you need to do a bit more planning.

How much stuff you have to move is the next consideration. Do you have only one rooms worth of furniture and belongings, or much more than that?

Estimates

If you have been living with your parents, you probably don't have a lot of furniture yet. In addition, after cleaning your closets and throwing out unwanted junk you have trimmed your belongings down to a manageable amount. Now you can call various moving companies and describe for them the quantity and approximate weight of all the objects you own. The mover will give you an estimate. If you have rooms full of furniture and additional boxes, they will send out an appraiser to give you an estimate. It is also a good idea to get estimates from several competitors.

Once you hear what they charge, you will probably abandon that idea and decide to rent a trailer or truck from one of the local or national one way rental companies. At least now you know how much you have to move when renting a truck.

Information

Knowledge is power, the power to save you a good deal of money. What you need to know at this point about packing, moving, storage, and many other facets of your operation to set up your household is contained within the wealth of information provided free of charge by many of the moving companies, both one way and national movers. Call or stop in and pick up this information. Subjects include: how to pack properly, ship plants, move pets, get insurance for your move, and many other topic areas. Check off lists for the last few weeks before the move are also provided by many of these companies.

Professional Movers

This is the best way to make a move if you have the money. Professional movers can do the whole thing. Pack all your belongings, ship them to your new home, and unpack them for you. This is the way life should be, however, you may have to ransom your grandmother to afford it. If you are moving to take a new job, see if your new employer will pay any of your moving expenses.

You need to confirm with the movers in advance exactly how much they get paid and when. There are horror stories of moving estimates that have doubled or tripled by the end of the move. The bottom line from the mover's standpoint, no money, no furniture.

One Way Rentals

The most common method (for those with limited budgets) for moving is to rent a trailer or truck to carry all your belongings.

Many rental companies like U-Haul or Ryder have free information to help you decide the best way to move. Anything you need to make the move easier can be purchased or rented including: packing boxes, packing materials, blankets, dollies, and ramps for loading.

If you rent a trailer, check your cars towing capacity to determine how large a trailer your car can safely pull. In addition, you may need to have a tow bar mounted to your car permanently, or if possible, rent a tow bar that can be taken on and off. A special plug needs to be connected to your car's light system in the rear so the brakes, turn signals, and parking lights will work on the trailer.

If your car is too small to tow a trailer you may need to rent a truck to carry your belongings. To tow the car, you need to rent a special rig that fits behind the truck. The rental cost of the tow rig and the decrease in miles per gallon will significantly change the cost of your move. Prepare your budget accordingly.

The Cost Of Moving

Finances certainly play a big part in your choice to move out on your own. It is a good idea to do a *moving budget* to find out how much your out-of-pocket expenses are going to be. Items for the budget might include: cost of truck or trailer rental, rigging light system for trailer, attaching tow bar to car, rental/purchase of packing items, preparation of car (i.e. tune up, mechanical check of all major systems), gas, tolls, motel, and food on the road. Check with all the local rental companies to come up with competitive rates.

Again, in the case of rental companies, you need to confirm your method of payment in advance. In addition, check into several items concerning your rental such as:

1) Is there a drop off fee for leaving the vehicle in another state?

2) Will your insurance company cover the trailer and your belongings while en route or will you need to get supplementary insurance through your carrier or the rental companies?

3) Will the rental company provide dollies, pads, and other items necessary for the move or must you rent them?

4) What is the basis of your rental fee for the truck or trailer? Is it based on mileage, the number of days you have the vehicle, or a combination of mileage and days rented?

5) Are there any penalties for going over a time limit or miles driven per day?

6) Can you get a price guaranteed in writing for the rental of the truck or trailer?

7) Who is responsible for repairs to the truck or trailer while en route to your new home? Do you pay for repairs and get reimbursed? Does the company have a road service for emergencies? Who pays for incidental expenses caused by any delays?

8) Renting the trailer during the week can insure your reservation and also may cost less. Certain times of the year also may be cheaper than others. Can the rental company give discounts for such times?

Some rental companies offer you help in determining the truck or trailer size needed to move your belongings. It is possible they have men for hire to help you move in case you need it. Be sure these men are covered by an insurance policy in case they drop your television or destroy some other piece of your property accidentally.

When moving yourself, you are responsible for packing and

loading not only the boxes but the trailer or truck you are using. Check with the company for information on how to do this correctly. Many rental companies have literature in brochure format covering every aspect of how to pack and properly load all of your belongings.

Alternate Methods

An alternate method of getting your belongings to your new home is to ship them through the U.S. Postal Service, UPS, or some other shipping service. I found this to be a convenient way to ship most of my belongings across the country. You need to have an address to ship the boxes to and someone to accept delivery if you are not there in time to accept delivery yourself.

Decisions, Decisions

What to do? No matter how you do it, making this move is going to cost you more than you want to spend. At this point, you may have more incentive to go back and delete a few more items to lighten the load. You also may want to check the possibility of storing some items with your parents until you can send for them or afford to have them shipped out to you.

Storage

The best of all possible worlds is being able to store your stuff with Mom and Dad. What if they are celebrating your finally moving out by selling the house and going on a world cruise? Who knows? For one reason or another you may have to check the possibility of storing your stuff at a commercial storage yard. Check out rates at this end and your final destination in case your apartment is not ready when you get there. It pays to have a fall back plan just in case.

Come Closer, Grasshopper

My personal philosophy is to travel as light as possible. Maybe, the world has changed but when I was just out of high school and college I did not have enough money to pay for these costs of moving. I was very good at creating a home by starting with card tables and folding chairs for my kitchen set, inflatable mattresses for my bed, lawn furniture for my living room, one pot and a frying pan to cook with, utensils snagged from fast food places, towels from the YMCA for the bathroom, and bookcases made out of boards and bricks. Now that was living. I called it Early Modern American Economic. The only other things I needed were my stereo boom box, my color TV, my video, and a phone. Who could ask for more?

You may want to give this philosophy some thought on your first move, Grasshopper.

Sit On Your Suitcase

Now that you have completed the basic planning and set up, it is time to start packing. The packing process will take quite some time. The best way to begin is to pack all non-essential items first. Get some boxes and begin packing everything you do not use on a daily basis. This will help alert you to how much trailer space or how many boxes you have to ship. Label each box clearly so you know what is inside each. If you don't label the boxes, you will have to search every one to find a suddenly necessary item. You know that item will be in the last box you look in no matter which box you start with.

As each week passes previous to your move, continue to pack any items that you will not need on a day to day basis. Throughout the packing process, you will be involved in other activities related to your move. It is to your advantage to remove as much clutter from your life as soon as possible.

CHAPTER 12:

GOOD-BYE!

Through all your planning, packing, and cleaning in preparation for your move, you pushed the thoughts of saying good-bye to friends and family to the back of your mind. The excitement of moving fills you with hope for the future, but the dread of leaving everyone you have known and loved over the years is almost too much to bear. Unfortunately, I have no great words of wisdom to comfort you with, or lessen your sense of loss. Moving is one big change, and change is thought by many to be one of the greatest stressors in life. You have given this move a great deal of thought and are determined to go through with it. Now you should deal with this aspect of your move, saying Good-bye, to help alleviate the stress this situation creates.

At least a month previous to your move, start visiting friends and acquaintances to begin the process of saying good-bye. You don't want to be rushed the day before the move with friends dropping over and no time to spend with them. You don't want the last impression they have of you to be interpreted as a brush off. It would seem insincere and that is the last thing you want them to think.

Plan a party for your friends. They may have (secretly) planned a going away party for you. In any case, invite them over to reminisce on all your shared escapades as a way of closing this aspect of your life. That doesn't mean you will never contact them again, or they will never visit, however, once you have moved away, the relationship will never be exactly the same again.

Write A Letter

With the expense of moving to a new home you may not be able to give the little mementos or presents to your friends that you would like. You can still give them something valuable, a personal note from yourself stating why you consider them to be such a good friend. In the letter, you can touch on some highlights you have shared. If you have some special object you know the person would like, you could present them with this item.

Get an address book to list all your friends phone numbers and addresses. Give your new address to your friends if you know it, or send it once you have moved in. Letters from family and friends are comforting when you are by yourself in a new environment. Make sure you also have the names and addresses of relatives and the various business associates you have come to know. That could be quite a number of people.

One suggestion is that you pack your hometown telephone book with the rest of your belongings. That way if you forget someone's phone number or need to call a business in your hometown area you won't have to spend a fortune calling information to find the number.

I'll Write You Every Day!

As you say your good-byes I am sure you will hear the comments "Make sure you write!"; "Send us your new address so we can drop you a line."; or maybe from a former lover, "I'll write you every day!" I've always wondered how anyone could come up with something new and interesting to write about every day.

Letter #362

Dear Studmuffin,
Today I had a salad and right now I am sending some lettuce to my big toe to keep it from being undernourished. Just a minute, I have to remember to take a breath.
Well, have to go now, I just remembered I have to clean the wax out of my ears. Write as soon as you can!
Love,
Babydoll

Encouraging Warm Regards

Seriously though, it is a good idea to stay in touch with all your friends. A technique called "encouraging warm regards" is an excellent idea. All you have to do is make a note when people's birthdays, anniversaries, or any special occasion is going to take place and send them a card. When your friends get the cards it causes them to think of you in warm and friendly ways. This technique is also a good idea for business associates. This practice keeps you in a favorable position so they think of you when special deals come down the road.

The Lowest Long Distance Rates

When they receive the letters or cards, your friends will have the urge to call you and talk about what is new with you. As you may remember from the section on budget, phone calls are one of the items that can cost you a bundle each month. Sending a letter right now is relatively inexpensive and since many people like to immediately gratify their wishes they may call you rather than taking the time to write a letter.

Most people like receiving letters and post cards from their friends. In some ways, it seems that letter writing is becoming a lost art. I know it always perks me up a bit to get a letter from a friend amongst the sea of bills I get in the mail everyday. Besides, if someday you do something really famous (or infamous), your letters could become worth a lot to historians.

Change of Address

Make certain to file a change of address form with the post office. This can be done before you leave or once you arrive at your new address. The U.S. Post Office has a change of address kit that you can pick up at any of their offices. On the form, you must indicate when you want your mail stopped at the old address and when you want delivery to begin at the new address.

Many businesses take two to three weeks to update their mailing lists. Notify anyone you do business with, magazine publishers, book of the month club, and others well in advance of the time you plan to leave. Ask a neighbor or your parents to collect any mail that comes after you leave and forward it to your new address.

The post office will forward all first - class mail for up to a year. Other packages and letters may be forwarded on your approval, however, depending on the class of mail, they may charge additional postage. (That means call Playboy or Cosmopolitan and have them forward your subscription.)

Some of the people, services, and businesses you will want to send change of address forms to are:

1) the post office

2) Internal Revenue Service (state and federal)

3) Credit card companies (gas, store, etc.)

4) attorney

5) accountant

6) doctor

7) dentist

8) veterinarian

9) insurance company (health, car, and life)

10) banks (especially if you have an outstanding loan) credit unions or finance companies (important if you are still making installments on your car)

11) stockbroker

12) employer (personnel office re: back pay, tax info)

13) any professional organizations you belong to

14) any clubs in which you are a member

15) subscriptions

16) selective service bureau

17) department of motor vehicles

18) church or synagogue

19) friends & relatives

20) business colleagues

21) voter registration

22) city or county tax assessor

23) your mom and dad.

Looking back over the list it is amazing how many people we come in contact with in our lives.

Terminate Services

At this point, you should notify anyone who does a service for you that you will be terminating their service on a particular date (i.e. paper boy, gardener, cleaner.)

Close Accounts

This is a good time to close accounts you have with local businesses and settle any outstanding balances. These accounts could include local stores where you have a charge card, video rental stores, a local supermarket, a bar tab, whatever. If you have any accounts in the bank like savings, vacation clubs, certificates of deposit, a safety deposit box, or anything needing your signature take care of these financial instruments at this time.

Keep your checking account active until you have settled into your new home. After opening a new checking account some banks require a two week hold on the deposit before you can make withdrawals. Stores may not accept a check from out of town, but you can pay your monthly bills with no problem or make deposits for new services. In addition, most ATM cards can now be used nationwide so you can withdraw cash from your account if necessary.

Utilities

Advise your phone, electric, gas, sewer, or trash services of the date each of these services should be discontinued.

Collect Records

I am not talking about musical records here, unless you have a collectors edition of the Brady Kids singing with Alvin and the Chipmunks. The records you need to collect before moving on include:

1) school records (high school and college transcripts, perhaps records for your child)

2) dental records and X-rays

3) medical records, X-rays, baseline mammogram (it is a good idea to get all of your current prescriptions refilled before moving, and get recommendations from your current doctors for a new doctor or dentist)

4) any veterinary records if you have a pet (update any shots or vaccines at this time)

5) collect all tax records and legal documents from your accountant and lawyer.

6) pay any local taxes (i.e. property, school, etc.) before you leave.

7) make sure your employer has your new address to send your W-2's if they do not have them ready to take with you.

8) ask your current employer for a letter of reference for future jobs.

This stage of the planning may take some time, so begin working on this area as soon as possible. The days are gone when you could throw a few things in a suitcase and just take off.

Transfer / Start Services

Depending on how far you move, you may be able to transfer some of your services without having to pay new deposits. In any case, based on the date of your move and ultimate arrival in your new home you will want to contact the services necessary for the basic enjoyment of life:

* electric   * trash

* phone   * water

* sewer   * oil

* cable TV   * gas

(begin newspaper delivery)

Let these companies know when you plan to occupy the premises so the services will be turned on (preferably the day before to be sure) when you get there.

Insurance

Contact your insurance agent to transfer coverage on your car to the new location as well as instituting "renter's insurance" to cover your belongings. Renter's insurance will cover your personal belongings but not the apartment or its fixtures. You might consider getting a liability policy in case you leave the stove on and start a fire while you are soaking in the tub.

Before moving out, you also should discuss your medical insurance situation and possibly vehicle insurance. Depending on your age and whether you are still in school, you may be able to stay on your parents' policy. Find out before you have an accident.

CHAPTER 13:

Load 'Em Up, And Move 'Em Out!

I am reminded of the old western movies where the trail boss moves among the covered wagons yelling at everyone to "Load 'em up, and move 'em out, Yee haw!" It is about time to hit the road, but before you do, let's stop and make sure you have everything prepared for the trip.

Travel Plans and Reservations

All you settlers who are just moseying over to the other side of town need not bother with this information. The rest of you pioneers, pay attention. Before hitting the road, you need to map out a route of travel for several reasons:

1) If some emergency should come up or a potential accident, your parents/friends have your planned route of travel so they can check to see if you are all right when you forget to check in with them.

2) You may want to make motel reservations in advance, especially if you travel on a weekend or holiday when the hotels and motels could be booked. Sometimes with advanced booking you can take advantage of special rates or offers.

3) Use a current road map to determine the quickest and easiest routes. Most maps have a legend that shows whether a road is a superhighway, interstate, surface street, or unfinished road. With this knowledge, you can determine the best route of travel to avoid poor road conditions.

Using the scale on the map (i.e. one inch equals ten miles), you can determine the length of any part of your journey. This is helpful when you want to figure out where you will be each day during the rush hour traffic. You can schedule your rest and meal breaks for this time. In addition, once you determine how fast you can safely travel while pulling a trailer, plus the amount of time you plan for breaks, you can then determine which towns you would like to stop in each night and reserve a room at a local motel.

Route Planning

It seems everyone is getting into the act from credit card companies, insurance companies, and the old stand by, the AAA. Many of these companies offer services like planning the best routes for you to take, emergency road service, bail bonds, and free towing. When you are on a tight budget, it is a good idea to have back up in case of a problem. Check with the Better Business Bureau and talk with friends and family about who they use and their experiences with each before deciding which company is best for your needs.

Service Your Car

Before taking your car on this trip you will want to take it to a trusted mechanic and have the whole car checked out. Check to be sure these items are in good working order:

1) brakes

2) tires properly inflated with sufficient tread

3) check all hoses and belts for wear and tear (if you have an older car you might want to purchase spares just to be sure)

4) check all fluid levels and top off as necessary (i.e. brake fluid, transmission fluid, oil, differential, radiator, windshield cleaner, water in battery, clutch master and slave cylinders)

5) change oil, air, and fuel filters

6) put in new spark plugs

7) have all joints lubricated

8) make sure the car drives in proper alignment.

This may be an extensive and expensive list, but not nearly as expensive as what it will cost you when you are out on the road stuck in a town called Eastern Ishkabibble. Then you will be at the mercy of some nefarious mechanic who can take advantage of you, especially if you have no knowledge of how your car works.

If you are unable to have these items taken care of by your mechanic, at least have him check each and tell you if any problem might develop. Then, you will know what to expect.

Basic Tool Kit

When you move into your new home, you will need some tools to set things up. You might as well put together a basic tool kit to keep in your car. A basic tool kit should have:

1) a pair of adjustable pliers

2) a set of wrenches (U.S. or metric depending on the vehicle) or at least two adjustable wrenches

3) a Phillips head screwdriver

4) a flat head screwdriver

5) a hammer

6) a knife

7) a roll of duct tape

8) a flashlight

9) a set of emergency road flares

10) keep a copy of the repair manual for your car with your tools, and anything else you feel is important.

Emergency Supplies

The most common problems to deal with on the road in relation to your car are overheating and tire trouble. Overheating may be caused by a ruptured hose, low radiator fluid, or a faulty thermostat. You can patch a rupture, once the hose has cooled, by wrapping it with duct tape. You should keep a container of anti-freeze/coolant to put in the radiator. Only replace the anti-freeze/coolant after the radiator has cooled sufficiently that you can remove the radiator cap without being scorched by hot steam. Do not fill a hot radiator with cool fluid, it might cause the radiator to crack creating an additional leak.

Before going on the road, make sure your spare tire is in good condition and properly inflated. Take the time to practice changing a tire. The worst place to learn how to change a tire is in the middle of a busy road with a loaded down car. If you don't want to chance changing a tire, auto supply shops carry a product that will inflate and plug a hole in a flat tire so you can make it carefully to the next service station where you can have the tire fixed properly. It is a good idea to have this product on hand in case of inclement weather or hazardous road conditions.

Munchies For The Road

Get yourself a cooler so you can put the food of your choice into it before you leave. Deli meats, bread, condiments, fruit, juice, peanut butter and jelly, or anything else you would like to eat during your journey. On the road you can stop and have a picnic. At the very least you can hold out longer while driving until you find some place with prices that at least enter the realm of reality. Breakfast and lunch are the easiest meals to prepare right out of your own chuck wagon, however, you should reward yourself at the end of a long day of driving by sitting down for a relaxed meal.

Traveler's Checks

When you are on the road, it is not a good idea to have a lot of cash on you. Everyone knows you are moving. Your car is packed or you are dragging a trailer, and that makes you an easy mark. Another reason is that with all the changes taking place daily as you drive to your new home, and the mess your car will eventually become, you might lose your money and not be able to find it. With travelers checks you can get them refunded at almost any bank branch around the country. Another option is to pay for everything with a credit card. This is a good idea for helping you to keep records of your moving expenses.

Captain's Log

"Using the light speed breakaway factor, I have eluded pursuit from authorities and saved two days travel time to my destination."

Like many people, if the speed limit sign says 55 I am usually doing 65. When you pull a heavy load behind you it is not a good idea to push the speed limit.

1) You will need longer stopping distances because the weight of the trailer will continue to push you forward. (Check into trailers with electric brakes.)

2) In an emergency situation, the trailer will make keeping control of your vehicle more difficult, excess speed will only add to that danger.

3) You will not save much time by pushing the speed limit. When I got my driver's license in Nevada, the driver's test manual listed the amount of time saved for every 5 mile per hour increment over the speed limit. I realized the amount of time saved was not worth the potential danger.

4) *"License and registration, please."* Getting pulled over for speeding is no fun. It is even less fun when you are from out of state. Unless you can prove you are actually moving to the state and setting up permanent residence you may be required to pay the fine on the ticket right then and there.

Tax Information

While traveling keep a log of how far you travel each day, your mileage, gas consumption, meals, and other expenses you incur while on the road. Once you are settled into your new home and are preparing your taxes you can use this information to write off the expense of your move.

Vital Documents

Keep all vital documents with you when traveling to your new home. These could include your driver's license, car registration, insurance papers, rental papers for trailer, bill of lading from mover, passport, apartment lease, or anything that may be vital to you over the first week or two as you move in to your new home.

The Last Check

When you are finally packed and about to leave you should perform one final check on your car (and trailer?).

1) Make sure everything is loaded so you have clear visibility out every window of your car. If you have a trailer, your side mirrors should enable you to see at least 500 feet behind you down either side of the car.

2) The load should be evenly distributed so the car or trailer does not obviously lean to one side or the other. Heavy items should always be on the bottom to help keep a lower center of gravity in the vehicle.

3) If everything is mechanically in order, make sure all your lights work properly (i.e. headlights, parking lights, turn signals, and emergency flashers.) Have someone stand outside your vehicle and check that all lights work on the car and the trailer.

4) Make sure the trailer is properly hitched to the car and safety chains are in place to keep the trailer from separating from your vehicle. Remember to remove all blocks from under the wheels before you drive away.

Just One More Thing

Wait just a minute, you have a few more things to do before you climb aboard and hit the road.

1. Confirm all your reservations.

2. Turn everything in the house off, unless of course your parents or other family members are still there using them.

3. Record time of departure and all utility meter readings.

4. Return the keys to the landlord (or parents).

5. Make sure your parents or a neighbor have your new address and will collect any mail delivered in the next few days.

6. If appropriate call the police to let them know you have vacated the premises and it is now empty.

7. Kiss the dog, the cat, the goldfish (blech!), your brothers and sisters, and finally your parents good-bye.

8. Re-confirm with your parents (or friends) what your travel plans are and when and how often you will contact them when you are on the road.

Using A Professional Mover

1. If you are using a professional mover make sure to get the driver's license number and the license number of the truck.

2. Confirm a method of contact with the driver for when you reach your destination. Give detailed directions and a map to your new home to the driver. Provide contact numbers with your parents or a friend in case of an emergency.

3. Confirm that your property is covered by insurance while in transit for damage, loss, or theft.

Pioneers Are The Ones That Get Stuck With Arrows

Well, pilgrim, you are about to become a pioneer of your own hopes, dreams, and lofty aspirations. You have planned every step of your move and it is time to hit the road. Remember, take your time getting there and always play it safe if there are uncertain driving conditions (i.e. weather, construction, accidents).

Don't pick up hitchhikers! The stories I could tell you, but never mind. It is not worth taking the chance. If anyone strange comes near you when you are on the road, get in your car and lock the doors and immediately (yet safely) drive away.

If you don't like driving alone, advertise in the paper for someone who is headed in the same direction. It can make the drive pass much quicker and you might develop a friend along the way.

See you when you get to your new home!

"Pioneers are the ones that get stuck with arrows."

CHAPTER 14:

Home Sweet Home

You made it! You are finally in your new home. The movers have dropped off all your stuff or you have unloaded the trailer and your new place is stuffed with packing boxes. Now to unpack all your boxes and put away all your stuff, change that disgusting wallpaper in the bathroom, and clean the bathroom and the kitchen.

Psyche!   Who are you, Felix Unger?

Rest and Relax

Sit back and catch your breath. Right now your apartment is full of boxes and everything is a mess. You just moved all your worldly belongings halfway around the earth, at least it seems that way. Relax and take a moment to rest. The boxes are not going anywhere. They will be there when you are rested and ready to unpack them.

R.I.P.

The first thing you should prepare is your bed. Unpack all your sheets and blankets, set your bed up where you want it, and make your bed. That way, if you do get the urge to start unpacking, you can drop into a coma on top of your already made bed when you are done.

Next, set up your television and your stereo. Now, go out and get yourself a meal at a restaurant (you deserve it) and then come back and relax for the rest of the evening.

Note: Make sure your appliances are at room temperature before you turn them on. If they have been out in the cold, immediate use could cause some damage.

Check Utilities

Having called the proper people, you may expect that all your services are turned on. Check to make sure. If they are not, immediately call and ask that they be turned on. Many apartment complexes already have the utilities turned on and will require that you have them transferred into your name within your first few days of occupancy.

Unpacking

Now that you have had time to rest and refresh yourself, it is time to unpack all your belongings. First, move each box into the appropriate room. If you marked each box, you know what it contains so this will be easy. You will probably want to unpack all your kitchen items first so you can prepare meals from this point on. No sense in wasting any left over travel money eating out all the time. The next room to unpack and set up is the bathroom. The rest of your belongings you can unpack as you desire.

Don't Change A Thing

Take some time to live in the apartment before you make any changes. What you do now you may decide to change back later. Also remember that any change you make in the apartment itself will have to be done with the permission of the landlord. That includes putting holes in walls to hang pictures, putting up extra towel racks in the bathroom, hanging plants, or putting in track lights.

Don't spend lots of money buying new furniture to fit this particular location. You may decide you don't like the apartment for one reason or another. Furniture and accessories to match the peach and purple motif of the current apartment may not fit in your next dream home.

Arranging the Furniture

Now is the time to decide what you are going to put where. If possible, have your moving men place the heavy pieces where you want them. If you are doing it with friends put the heavy items in the most likely places before your friends split and call it a day.

Furniture Rental

In an earlier chapter, you were given lists of all the possible items you may want to furnish your new home. Right now you probably have all the basics but could use additional furnishings to make it feel like a home. Try renting furniture to get an idea of what you will ultimately want. In almost every major metropolitan area, there are several furniture rental stores. Each store contains a wide assortment of furniture displayed with complementary room pieces that you can rent on a monthly basis. Everything you need can be rented, and possibly rented with the option of buying at some point in the future.

Garage Sales & Auctions

Remember, garage sales are a great way to get bargains on furniture and many other household items. You can also look in your apartment complex mail room and laundry rooms for notices of people moving out who want to sell pieces of furniture.

Keep an eye on the classified ads for estate auctions and

business auctions. Many times they are selling new or near new office furniture for extremely low prices and all sorts of items that have been collected in bankruptcies, foreclosures, and repossessions. Many of these items are being sold on a cash basis for as much as they can get at that moment. Creditors want to recoup their losses and don't want to pay storage fees on the items in question. Give them a low, yet reasonable offer, and you may walk away with everything you need to furnish the apartment.

Check Out The Town

Before you go on a buying spree, check out your new town and see what it has to offer. You may decide you really like it, or you may decide to move to another area or out of town all together.

Once you have settled in, a fun way to get to know your way around is to hop in your car and start to drive. See how far you can go and how many turns you can take and still make it back to your apartment without getting lost. Obviously, you want to find the local supermarket, drug store, hardware and home supplies, the local movie theater, the churches or synagogues, and all the utility companies, banks, post office, and other businesses you will now be using.

You may want to get a street map from a local gas station and mark off the location of all the businesses that you frequent so you can establish a traffic pattern that is efficient and wastes less of your time while out shopping or running errands.

Emergency Phone Numbers

Now that you call this place home, be sure to find and list all the appropriate numbers for emergency services (i.e. police, fire, ambulance).

CHAPTER 15:

Getting To Know You

The excitement of making the move is over and you begin to settle into your new home. You decide to go and visit your friends. Wait a minute! Your friends are halfway across the state or halfway across the country! Even if you still live in the same town you are probably not going to see all your buddies at Brother's Pizza every night. The friendly grocer at the corner store is not there any more, because now you shop at different places and see new faces.

Your friends will develop new association patterns now that you have left a void in one aspect of their lives. So what can you do? All right, let's watch a little television. Boring! Nothing is on you want to watch anyway. You are a people person and want to be around somebody, anybody. Remember, you can't use the phone too much or you will build up a whopping phone bill every month. So what are you going to do?

Where to Make Friends

In some towns, they may still have a version of the "Welcome Wagon" where townsfolk come out to meet new residents and make them feel welcome. Newcomer's clubs are also beginning to pop up where you can go to meet new people and make friends as well as get involved in activities like: gardening, bridge, hikes, dances, and monthly luncheons.

Other ways to meet new people and get involved in your new community include:

1) Church or religious groups

2) Community service organizations (Jaycees, Kiwanis, Chamber of Commerce, etc.)

3) Singles columns and dating services

4) Sports participation (i.e. joining local basketball league, jogging clubs, etc.)

5) Working out at a fitness club

6) Donating time to volunteer organizations (i.e. helping at hospitals, teaching people to read, working with the homeless, doing fund raising projects)

Several activities are listed in the "Community" section of the local newspaper. The activities around town include: nature walks, concerts in the park, museum tours, and special interest groups giving demonstrations. Get involved and you are sure to meet lots of people.

Making Friends At Work

Obviously, at your new job, you can meet a whole new group of people, many whom you may choose to call friends. Remember that making a real friend takes lots of time together and many shared experiences. You will not be able to replace lifelong friendships overnight. Take your time and get involved and always act friendly to those you live and work with and many friendships will grow spontaneously.

Your Home Is Your Castle

Before you invite people over remember that your home is your castle. It is the place you go to get away from the confusion and hassle of the work world. If you invite everybody over to your apartment to get to know them better, they may decide your place is their new hang out. If you value your privacy make sure you set some ground rules (i.e. call before dropping over, leave at a reasonable hour). You also may want to let some of your new friends know that your place is not Joe's Bar & Grill. Friends who eat you out of house and home are questionable friends.

CHAPTER 16:

Financial PMS
(this PMS knows no gender)

The phone is ringing. A sensation of dread overcomes you as you decide whether to answer the phone or screen the call with your answering machine. Finally, the answering machine takes the call and sure enough it is a creditor wondering when you are going to make your payment that is now past due.

Past Due

For many, the thought of dealing with a creditor is at best extremely uncomfortable and for some, downright intimidating. Visions of evil men who assassinate babies come to mind. The thought of a few brutes smashing your face into hamburger meat, or possibly the thought of a lawyer dragging you into court summon dark imaginings about what could happen to you. Perhaps you will be thrown in jail, or placed into slavery for the rest of your life. None of this is true, it is just your imagination.

All right, maybe you skipped the chapter on budgeting your finances, or some catastrophic situation occurred that put you behind financially. Whatever the reason, you have not paid your bills and now you need to deal with a creditor. What should you do?

Dealing with Creditors

When a creditor calls, as they usually will, when you are past due in your payments, they are calling to find out where your payment is and when they can expect to receive it. The key to dealing with creditors is:

1) Be honest.

2) Follow through with any promises you make.

Creditors are people like you and me (they sometimes make mistakes) and most are willing to help you out if you are straight with them and let them know your situation. Sometimes due to an emergency, if you fall behind in payments, they may defer a payment or two and add these payments to the end of your loan. This will allow you, for the present, to get back on your feet. There may be a fee for such a service but that is a small price to pay when you are financially strapped.

Obviously, what a creditor can or cannot do will depend on the type of credit (car loan, credit card, furniture purchase) you have with them. Credit card companies may accept a partial payment whereas a company financing your car may not.

Types Of Credit

Credit comes in different forms. One form of credit is called **collateralized**. For instance, suppose you buy a car and finance it through a credit company. The car will be used as the collateral to secure the loan. The creditor will come and repossess the car if you can't make your payments. In this case, the creditor does not have to accept a partial payment because you have legally given him the right to take the car if you default in your payments.

Credit cards are considered **an unsecured loan.** If you can't make your payment, the creditor may allow you to make partial payments for a short time until you can catch up. Even though you make partial payments, the creditor may still notify credit reporting agencies. The creditor may do so without telling you which can in turn affect your future ability to get credit.

What To Do

DO NOT IGNORE YOUR CREDITORS!

Regardless of your situation do not ignore your creditors. In fact, it is best that you *contact your creditor first* when you are experiencing financial difficulty. Any creditor will be more willing to work with you if you call them before you become delinquent in your payments. It shows them you are attempting to be financially responsible.

When you talk with creditors, always be polite. Many of the questions they ask are not meant to be intrusive. The creditor or his agent is only trying to determine how he may best serve the situation. Keep in mind it is his job to collect on your outstanding debt. In the final analysis, you are the one that borrowed and agreed to pay the money back in a specific manner. The creditor may not have to work with you, so it is to your advantage to be as helpful and courteous as possible when determining payment arrangements.

Explain your situation as succinctly as possible. If you can make a payment, tell the creditor how much and when they can expect to receive it. Then make sure they receive it on that date! Stringing them along with promises that are not kept will only hasten the time when a notice from a lawyer demanding payment appears. The next step is a sheriff who knocks on your door to give you a "writ of possession" from your creditor, stating he is repossessing your merchandise.

It Won't Matter

Don't be fooled into thinking you can outrun your credit history. Unfulfilled obligations will show up as a "charge off" that will appear on your personal credit report for the next seven to ten years, and that will certainly affect your ability to get credit.

Loans With Bad Credit = $ Big Interest $

You may think that you have beaten the system because you still get loans or credit. You also may be paying a very high premium. Once a creditor sees a series of late payments or delinquencies he may still issue you credit. He will do so charging you the highest amount of interest he can to offset the chance of your not repaying the loan. In this scenario, you pay *twice the interest* of a person with good credit.

The key is, whatever credit you have, pay it on time.

Credit Reports

Keep on top of your credit rating by sending away to any of the major credit reporting agencies (i.e. TRW, Equifax, Trans Union) and ask for a copy of your credit history. There is a cost for this service ($20 or more). The cost is worth it to see what your rating is and if there are any erroneous entries declaring you have less than a respectable credit history.

If you dispute something on your credit history you can contact the creditor in question and have them make the necessary changes. You also can file a DF (Dispute Form) with the credit reporting agency and have them check into any discrepancies. You may be able to have a consumer comment placed on your report about any information you dispute. In any case, it is a good idea to check on your credit report at least once a year.

Locked Out

"Wilma, let me in!" Banging on the door of your apartment to get back inside may work if it was your pet dinosaur that locked you out, however, if it was your Godzilla-like landlord you may be spending a cold night on a park bench.

The Rent Is Due

One of the most important payments you make each month is your rent. This payment should always be made *on time*. Renters who are chronically late in their payments stand the chance of one day losing their apartment to someone else whose ability to pay is more certain.

Connect The Dots

The following series of events are the steps taken by a landlord before you are locked out of your apartment. Interrupting any one step will keep the final picture of you on a park bench from being completed.

Before your rent payment is late, talk to the apartment manager to make arrangements for paying what you owe. The manager may give you several days, usually up to the tenth of the month, to pay your rent. For this service, they may tack on a late penalty to your rent.

If the rent is not paid by this time, the landlord may file a legal statement with the local township to begin eviction proceedings. At this point you will have five working days from receiving the notice of eviction to contest the action. You will need a reason for contesting the action such as the refrigerator doesn't work, or the heater is broken. In any case, to stop the proceeding, you will be asked by the local government to place the rent money into an escrow account to be held until repairs are made.

It will cost you to file against the landlord once they have started eviction proceedings. However, once you do contest the action the landlord may not hassle you for any reason to collect the rent.

If you have no plausible reason for contesting the landlord's action, the eviction procedure will continue with a court date set ten days to two weeks after the filing. At this point a judge may order you to vacate the premises in which case you may only have twenty - four hours to move your belongings and leave.

Paying your rent in full at any time may stop the eviction proceeding. However, the landlord can begin those proceedings again from that point if he is determined to get you out.

If for some reason you are evicted and a lock is put on your door, you can still get in to remove your belongings by contacting the apartment manager. If, however, you abandon your furniture and leave it behind, the apartment manager may sell it after thirty days to help recoup his loss on the rent.

Each township, city, or state has its own rental laws peculiar to that area. The thoughts and ideas listed here are generalizations to give you an idea what could happen. Check with your local township for the specific laws that will affect you.

Your Rap Sheet

Once evicted, just like bad credit, a notice will be added to your credit files that will follow you around wherever you go in search of another apartment. A notice like that can mean the difference between getting an apartment or having your rental application politely returned.

If the reason for eviction was failure to pay, a new landlord may require a substantial deposit and a few months rent to protect himself in case you are again unable to pay.

Keep the lines of communication open with your apartment manager and always pay your rent on time.

Summary

If you are experiencing financial difficulty:

1) Contact the creditor before payment is delinquent and discuss any options (i.e. deferred payments, partial payments, changing payment date, etc.)

2) Be honest about your situation. Communicate openly so the creditor can be of maximum help in getting you back on track.

3) If you make a promise of payment, on a specific date, follow through.

4) If you have trouble with a creditor and are unable to resolve it yourself, do not ignore the situation. Contact the Better Business Bureau or any government agency that can help. If this does not work, discuss the situation with someone your trust. If you are served legal papers you may want to discuss the situation with a lawyer, however, that could be more expensive than paying the debt.

Remember, you are responsible to repay any credit that is extended to you promptly. The results of not keeping to your agreements can follow you around for years and have a profound effect upon your life. Don't let your credit get out of hand in the first place.

Personal Note

Like many others, I learned the hard way. I made mistakes and fouled up my credit. The most important thing I learned during those times was that I was still a worthwhile individual. Even if you follow the best advice, situations will still occur that put you behind financially. Initially, you may feel down, but after you have had a good cry, just keep right on doing the best you can.

CHAPTER 17:

Paying The Piper

Death and taxes. You have to pay taxes and you will certainly die someday. I don't want to spend a lot of time talking about dying. When you are gone it won't matter to you anyway, everyone else has to clean up your mess. However, when you move, you should update your will to reflect the laws of the state where you live. Life is stranger than fiction and it is possible everything could, by some fluke, be left to your pet goldfish. Just imagine the stress you will cause the poor fish, deciding what size tank it should move into, choosing between the deluxe model sunken castle or a tasteful rock garden with coral, and of course a fake diver to put out front to impress the neighbors.

The Tax Man

Taxes - the dreaded subject. Nobody likes to talk about taxes except to gripe, and certainly nobody likes to take the time to fill out their yearly tax returns; it is too much work.

Your parents may have filled out your return in years past, or included you on theirs, but now it is very important that you take the time to file a return every year and do it correctly. A mistake made now may not be found until years later during an audit. The IRS adds penalties and interest to back taxes to motivate you to pay them on time in the future.

Now that you live on your own you need to keep track of

receipts and expenses that can be deducted from your tax liability for the year. In addition, the amount of tax you have to pay will affect your budgeting for the month and year. I used to get my tax returns in early so I could use my return to pay some bills. If this is the case in your situation, then like myself, you probably need to work on budgeting a bit better.

Who Needs To File?

As of this writing, any single individual making over $6050 a year must file. Married couples making over $10,900 are also required to file a tax return. Even children making over $600 a year in interest income must report these earnings on their parent's tax return.

If you are still in school and your parents claim you as a dependent, you can earn up to $3700 a year without having to pay taxes. The amount of money you earn before you must pay tax changes every year, so check with a local IRS office for current figures.

Lost Money?

A possibility might exist that the government owes you some money. If, in the past, you have held several jobs while you were in school, and your employer deducted federal income tax (as he should), you may be able to recover those taxes. Many young people do not file returns, assuming they don't have to because they have earned under the limit prescribed by the IRS. That may be true, however, if you don't file you will never receive a return on the taxes the government has already collected from your paychecks.

Check your W-2 forms for the past few years to see how much has been deducted. You may find that you can file a return and receive a refund from the IRS.

Just Married

If you just got married and changed your name, contact the social security office to make sure that taxes withdrawn from your pay are being properly applied to your account.

A Look In The Mirror

Many people dread doing their taxes because it forces them to look back over the year and see all they have done or all they wanted to do but never accomplished. It can be tough to look at all the hopes and aspirations that never materialized. Also, if the individual has not been budgeting and planning properly, tax time may cause a major crunch in his/her finances.

It is important that you keep accurate records of all your expenses and income. Simply placing a shoe box on a shelf and collecting all your receipts is a first step. To make life less difficult at the end of the year, you can organize your receipts every three months. This also will keep you in tune with your tax situation come April 15th.

Burning The Midnight Oil

Personally, I can't stand doing my own tax return. Half the time I can't even understand it. If you have little in the way of expenses and not much income to report, you may be fine filling out one of the IRS's "EZ" income tax reports. If, on the other hand, you have been acting the young entrepreneur, dabbling in a business venture, it is in your best interest to let a professional do your returns. There are several tax preparation services that will make sure your taxes are done correctly and you are not over or underpaying your taxes.

(Tax forms are available by calling the IRS or you can pick them up at any post office or library.)

CHAPTER 18:

The Toilet Seat Is Up!

After living on your own for a few months or even a year or more, you may find that your bills are starting to pile up. Having kept good records you know that you have not been living beyond your means, however, inflation and rising costs have slowly whittled down your financial safety margin. Unexpected bills have popped up along the way to cut down your savings even more. Moving back home is an extreme last resort, if it is a possibility at all. The choices you have left seem to be: win the lottery, get another job, cut down your costs (you could stop eating), or find a roommate to split the expenses.

I Now Pronounce You...

The best thing about living on your own is that you can do anything, whenever you want, without having to answer to anyone else. You have a certain amount of anonymity when you live in a large apartment complex, with complete freedom to come and go as you choose until you begin to share your home with someone else.

Taking on a roommate to help lower expenses can be like getting married. Bear with me and I will explain. Unlike riding in an airplane, I will ask you not to place your mind in an upright and locked position for takeoff into my next flight of fantasy.

"I Think, Therefore I Am Single"

You get home from work. Once inside the door you toss your coat on the couch and throw your papers from work on the table. You open the refrigerator and drink milk straight from the carton. Dishes are in the sink from sometime before Christmas (it's now March), so you only wash what you need to heat a can of Spaghettios and eat some leftover pizza from two days ago.

There are no worries about cleaning the apartment. Why clean the shower as long as there is a white circle in the bottom of the tub that you can stand in? The bedroom has a sculpture made of tossed underwear that hasn't been cleaned in a few weeks. It gives the room a certain ambience, but otherwise the room looks fine. Dustballs that look like little tumbleweeds blow across the room whenever there is a draft, but why vacuum when you can knit them into sweaters when they get bigger?

You can look like Attila the Hun all morning if you want before leaving for work. Running around in a bathrobe or in the buff is perfectly okay.

Now doesn't this sound much better than having someone around who doesn't live the same way you do? Bringing in a roommate can be like getting a spouse. Shortly after this person (spouse or roommate) moves in he/she wants to change everything to fit his/her lifestyle. Pretty soon the toilet has a ski cap and a little welcome mat in front. The silly person even puts a little sweater on the tissue box. One sure sign of an imminent change in your lifestyle is when you find dried flowers and bushes hanging from the walls.

All the delights like eating a half gallon of ice cream for dinner will disappear. Socks left on the floor, in the mind of this significant other, can cause an imbalance in the earth's crust (if they are not immediately placed in a hamper) sending shock waves and earthquakes to devastate parts of the world. Isn't your life better the way it is right now, even if you have to live in poverty?

The captain has put on the seat belt sign. We hope you have enjoyed this flight. We will be landing and returning to reality shortly. (Back off Dr. Freud, it was just a story!)

Infinite Diversity Infinite Combinations *(a Vulcan Philosophy)*

All right so you don't have to be Sherlock Holmes to figure out the last example was male/female oriented. I just didn't trust what my imagination might come up with for male/male or female/female situations. I'll let you come up with your own sordid ideas.

Seriously, everyone has their own style of living. Some of us are night owls, while others get up at the crack of dawn. Some of us squeeze the toothpaste in the middle and others roll it up from the bottom. The potential for difference is higher than the chance of getting a roommate who is similar. The question is, can you live with this person and any character quirks he/she may have?

Choosing a roommate should be a well thought out and defined process. After all, you will see this person every day and every night for the foreseeable future once they move in.

Before deciding on a roommate, check with your landlord about subletting parts of your apartment or having the new renter added to your lease. Also remember that you are responsible for any damage done to the apartment by your new tenant. Make sure you have appropriate renters insurance and liability coverage just in case.

Wanted: Single White Female
(greens and blues okay, absolutely no purples)

Exactly what are you looking for in a roommate? The best place to start is to define what it is you like to do and what your lifestyle is like.

1) What kind of music do you like?

2) What are your favorite foods?

3) What are your favorite television shows?

4) What sports, hobbies, or activities do you enjoy?

5) What do you do for a living?

6) When do you get up to go to work each day?
(When do you get home?)

7) What are your goals and aspirations?

8) What kind of clothes do you wear?

9) What is your social life like?

Obviously, this is not an all-inclusive list, but it will give you a starting point so you can find a roommate that complements those attributes.

To find a roommate, start by asking friends that have voiced the desire to move out. Maybe, someone at your work place is looking for a place to live. If you live in a college town, you might want to take in a student for part of the year to supplement your income. The beauty here is that you may have your place all to your self over the summer. The other advantage is that students are fairly transient, so they are less of a problem to get out if undesirable circumstances arise. If all else fails, you can always place an ad in the newspaper or in one of the apartment rental magazines.

Just The Facts, Ma'am

When deciding who will be your new roommate, rely on your gut instincts and always do a background check. You should have each prospective tenant fill out an application form that includes their name, address, phone number, current place of business, personal references, and as much credit history as you can check out. Find out as much as you can up front rather than getting a surprise down the road when they tell you they can't pay the enormous phone bill they have built up.

Like your apartment manager, you may want to have your prospective tenant pay a security deposit as well as a months rent in advance. Keep the finances strictly on a business level regardless of whether this is a friend or co-worker you have known for some time.

The Hand That Rocks The Cradle

An important issue may be deciding who is in control. Everything from deciding whether to add this person to a lease, or onto any utility bills, and who makes the payments is vital. Since you are the original tenant, you may feel that decisions should ultimately be made by you, however, this may not turn out to be the case. Once firmly entrenched in your household, a new roommate could begin to make your life a living hell.

Coming home after a hard day at the job, you may be thinking of sitting back and relaxing in front of the television only to find your roommate and a date making out on your new couch. Maybe, you left a container of frozen yogurt in the freezer for dessert only to find that it has been consumed. *(Hope the dog didn't get it!)*

Pre-Nuptials

The potential conflicts that can arise when you take on a roommate are many. To keep these annoyances to a minimum, you should outline a co-habitation contract. This contract should cover all the details of day to day life. For example:

1) What payments are due and when?

2) Who pays the monthly bills?

3) Can you borrow each others things?

4) Who is responsible to keep basic foods stocked in the refrigerator (i.e. butter, eggs, milk, ketchup, etc.)?

5) Will each person have his or her own shelves in the refrigerator and specifically designated cabinets?

6) Who cleans and vacuums the apartment? Is it done on a rotation basis? What happens if it is not done?

7) Can each person invite over friends anytime of the day or night? Can they sleep over?

8) Who decides what gets watched on television in the main room or played on the stereo? What is an appropriate sound level?

9) Will one of you take a shower the night before or is it catch as catch can in the bathroom every morning?

10) Who gets the parking spot in front of the apartment?

11) Must you develop a system to check in with your roommate or continue to live your life as you please?

12) What are the cooking arrangements? Each cooks his/her own or will you go in on some items to lessen your expenses?

13) Do dishes need to be cleaned right away or can they stay in the sink overnight?

14) What method will be used to resolve disputes if you and your roommate can't see eye to eye?

Cracking The Books

The preceding information also may apply if you share a dormitory room at college. It is difficult to study if your roommate invites over friends to help polish off a case of beer. Tailor the information presented for your own needs.

Talk Is Cheap

Whatever financial and living arrangements you make, write them out and have your new roommate sign the agreement. What he/she tells you up front to get his/her foot in the door and what really happens down the road may be two different things. It is better to have your agreements in writing.

Note: You might want to use a standard lease form available at most office supply and stationery stores.

"Why clean the shower as long as there is a white circle in the bottom of the tub that you can stand in?"

CHAPTER 19:

Too Good To Be True

It is an unwritten law that if it sounds too good to be true it probably is. Once you have established a place of your own you will find you are deluged with offers from all over. Credit card companies will send you pre-approved credit, people will call you on the phone to tell you that you are the guaranteed winner of at least:

A) *a color TV*

B) *a brand new car*

C) *a trip for two to Hawaii*

D) *$2000 in cash*

Everybody and their brother (brothers always get a bum rap) will contact you to get you to buy whatever it is they have to sell. Often, it is only so much hot air, which is okay if you are having a birthday and need someone to blow up the balloons.

You may think "Wow! I'm somebody now. Look at all the people who want to do business with me." Believe this, they only want to part you from your money. Many of these people get your name and address from other businesses who sell your name for a profit from their in-house mailing list. That's right. Almost any business you patronize and give your name and address to is going to continue to profit from their association with you by selling your name to various mailing lists throughout the country. Once your name gets on these lists it is circulated far and wide. You will receive literally tons of mail for the rest of your life offering you eternal youth products, bust developers, instant hair growth, lingerie ads, department store catalogs, and every get rich quick scheme you can imagine.

Do the planet a favor. Save a few trees by returning all the offers unopened to the local recycling center. As stated earlier, they are, in most instances, too good to be true.

Get It In Writing

When you move out you will be involved in a variety of transactions. These transactions may be in the form of signing lease agreements for an apartment, buying a car, and getting credit for new furniture. On each document, you are required to sign your name as legal proof of your intent to be bound by the agreement.

Unfortunately, many individuals are unscrupulous and will take advantage of you. Deals based on their good word or a handshake are almost always a con job, a way of getting you to purchase based on non-existent benefits. These same individuals, however, will protect their interests and require you to sign statements outlining what you owe them and when.

I have been offered special deals only to find out that some fictitious manager could not approve it, or an item was sold out and only the next higher priced model was available. Other instances include being told by a landlord that my carpet would be cleaned before I moved in, and it wasn't. In a perfect world, I am sure each of these people would like to follow through on their promises, unfortunately this world is full of unfulfilled promises.

Many people accept these bargains or agreements as the selling point that helps them decide to purchase. When push comes to shove and we want the seller to back up his word, we are invariably directed to read the fine print. The fine prints says representatives of the company cannot make special offers without authorization from the company. Many of these hucksters in reality do not make these offers, however, they carefully prepare their sales presentations to make it seem that the benefit discussed is included in the offer.

The Bottom Line

Regardless of what anybody says, when you are putting your name on the line, buying, leasing, or renting anything make sure **"ALL THE TERMS"** are clearly explained and written on the agreement. This document should be dated and clearly state what is being offered and the time limit you have to accept such an offer.

In fairness, we all have different styles of communication. One person could simply be talking about possibilities, while the person listening could be interpreting these "possibilities" as promises. It happens. Once, I went to pick up my new car and found the price to be higher than I had originally agreed upon. When the salesman and I were talking about how good the car would look with tinted windows, he took it upon himself to have the windows tinted. He tried to badger me into paying for the window tint, but in the end I drove away not a penny poorer.

To save yourself a headache always demand the details of any agreement or business transaction be clearly stated and reduced to written form. If you have any question about the agreement, check it out with someone you trust such as your parents or a specialist in that particular field. If the person you are doing business with will not agree to this, it is a sure sign you should not be involved with them in the first place.

Note: Regardless of what you are told, never place your signature on any document that has any blank spaces on it. Your signature should only be placed on documents where every item is completely filled in and you agree with the contents of those items. Blank spaces can be filled in later by unethical persons who can hold you accountable for whatever they have written since your signature says you agreed to it. In a court of law, it would be your word against theirs and they have a document signed by you! Simply scratch out or place the symbol NA which means "not applicable" in any area that is left blank. No matter what the transaction, get all the particulars in writing and signed by the person authorized to make such agreements.

Master The Moment

Whatever you do, ***DO NOT, I repeat DO NOT ever give your credit card number over the phone*** to take advantage of a "special" offer. Credit card scams are all over the country and take many forms, many of which sound plausible but usually end up with you getting nothing of value in return. The worst case scenario is that now these people have your name and card number as well as expiration date and can begin charging all sorts of things to your card and you may be held liable to pay for them.

Tracking down the perpetrators of these schemes is difficult because they can set up shop with one phone line anywhere. In addition, they can be gone instantly with very little loss on their part if the authorities arrive. If you find you must have something offered over the TV, radio, or in a phone solicitation pay for the item using a postal money order that can be tracked. The U.S. Postal Service will track down dishonest people who commit mail fraud. Additionally, using a postal money order does not give out any information about your bank account.

> ***"If it sounds to good to be true, it probably is."***

CHAPTER 20:

Time Management

Buzzzzz!

Hmmm? (Mumble, mumble) Ooh baby, I love it when you do that!

BUZZZZZZZZZZZZZZZZZZZ!

"What? Oh, my God I've overslept again!"

During the next few minutes you look like the Mad Hatter as you run around trying to prepare for work and concoct some excuse you hope your boss will believe.

One of the joys of living on your own is staying up or out all night and doing whatever you want. One of the responsibilities is getting everything done you are supposed to do on time. That includes getting up on time for work every morning, making sure reports are done on time, scheduling time for haircuts, paying your bills, vacuuming the carpets, cleaning your clothes, going out with your significant other, planning your meals, shopping, balancing your check book, get the idea!

Parkinson's Law - *Work expands so as to fill the time available for its completion.*

Keeping in mind Parkinson's Law, you will need to budget your time wisely so you use only that which is needed to accomplish your tasks. That way the rest of your time can be used in the pursuit of hedonism, wanton lust for life, and watching your favorite television shows.

Keeping Pace

Emergencies are what happen when you let little projects accumulate until they become big projects that had to be done yesterday. Mostly emergencies are a lack of preparation on your part for dealing with your responsibilities. Everyone on this planet gets only twenty - four hours a day to accomplish what they want to do. The difference in what each of us is capable of doing depends on our ability to prepare for activities that focus on our most desirable goals.

Chart Your Activities

To find out how you are spending your time, keep a record of your daily activities over the next month. Use the forms in the back of this book (blank calendar, and daily "to do" sheets) to track your activities and determine if you are using your time in the most productive manner. Using the calendar, track the activities that you must take care of each month. For example, every other week you may need to spend some time paying your bills, or doing your laundry, or cleaning your house. Other activities may take place once a week like taking out the trash or buying groceries.

On the daily "To Do" sheets you can track your activities for each day of the week. The easiest is marking off when you go to work and when you come home. On certain days, you may work out at the health club, or take a class at the college. List everything you do on a regular basis on each of these days.

After you have tracked your activities for a month, you will have a good idea of what your life is like in weekly chunks of time.

122

Remember, the purpose of tracking is not to fill your schedule with lots of activities, but to find out how you currently spend your time. A good question to ask of each activity; "Is it goal achieving or simply tension relieving?" Sometimes when I sit at my desk to do some writing I find that I procrastinate by taking care of miscellaneous paperwork first. It feels as though something is being accomplished, but in reality it is just paper shuffling. I am not achieving my goal to finish a chapter or begin a new article. Being active is not the same thing as being productive.

Review your goals and make sure they are current and specific. Compare what your goals are to how you are spending your time daily. Are you doing at least one thing each day to move you in the direction of your most dominant goals? If not, re-evaluate how you spend your time and focus on your priorities.

> *"Being active is not the same thing as being productive."*

CHAPTER 21:

Burning Your Bridges

Independence is a heady feeling. Finally out on your own and able to do anything you please any time you please, right? Now, you may feel you can tell some people from your past exactly what you think of them. Maybe your parents, brothers, or sisters drove you crazy and still do, and now you feel that you can put them in their place.

I urge you to reconsider. Whatever the reason you have for moving out, make sure you *leave on good terms* with everyone. That may be difficult but it can have positive consequences for the future.

After all the planning, new skills, and ideas you have learned while preparing to move out, you must make room for the possibility of emergencies, catastrophic error on your part in the financial realm, and plain old bad luck.

Follow along with this scenario. All your bills are up to date and you have purchased the last of the items you need to call your new place home. For the next few months everything is going fine. The following week you take your car in to the shop and find out you need new brakes and two new tires. The mechanic tells you the repair bill is at least $500. A quick perusal of your savings and checkbook reveals that you have a total of $235, and your next pay check is not for a week and a half.

What are you going to do? The famous standby everyone thinks of is Mom and Dad - of course they will bail you out.

Suddenly, a flood of memories pour through your mind reminding you of how you told your parents in a heated moment how prepared you were and that nothing was going to go wrong. Who knows, you might have gone even farther and ostracized them from your life.

What happens now when you come crawling back begging for help with your financial difficulties? If you have really great parents, they may understand you were just blowing off steam. If you have the kind of parent that says, "let the kid learn from his own mistakes," in the long run you may be better off for the experience, but you won't feel any better in the present. If you really blew it, your parents may not even acknowledge you.

Remember Murphy's most famous law *"If anything can go wrong, it will at the worst possible moment."* Situations occur where you need the help of family, friends, bosses, co-workers, and neighbors. If you are prone to telling people off and burning your bridges in an attempt to assert your independence, you may find yourself stuck with no where to turn for help in your crisis situation.

I am not going to tell you how to handle your personal affairs. Sometimes, it is necessary to blow off steam, however, when you first move out it helps to be on good terms in all your relationships. In addition, it is a good idea to lend a helping hand when possible to your friends, family, and co-workers.

Remember the revised Golden Rule:

"Do unto others as they would like to be done unto."

Follow that rule when dealing with others and you will find lots of people there to help you when you need a hand.

CHAPTER 22:

Happy Trails To You...

Hopefully, I have given you some ideas that have been helpful as you made the move into your new home. Now and then you might want to page through this book again to refresh yourself on some ideas that you have forgotten.

Congratulations on having made the move and living the life that you choose. I hope everything works out for you! I would love to hear your comments or suggestions for future editions of this book. Please write to me care of the publishers address.

"Live Long and Prosper."

APPENDIX A:

WIN Notebook

Many people intend to achieve their goals. Unfortunately, they tend to backslide because they do not follow through with the habits that bring them success. Now that you have started on a program that will help you organize yourself to achieve your goals I suggest that, if successful, you continue to use these ideas. Each of these forms can be placed in a three ring binder and separated by sections according to your need. This can in effect become your WIN notebook. Keeping a notebook will remind you of your goals and aspirations. Writing down everything that works will allow you to create your own blueprint for success that you may one day want to share with others.

Here are two more ideas that will help you in your quest to live life on your own terms.

Bubble Maps

Getting started with a project is difficult because you have no idea where to begin. I have found that using "bubble maps" sometimes helps. A bubble map is created when you take a piece of paper and throw down whatever idea comes to you about one of your goals. As you write down each idea you simply circle it creating a bubble. As further ideas pop into your head write them down and circle them on the paper. There is no order as to how or where you write the ideas on this page.

When you are done, your sheet will have lots of bubbles on it with ideas inside. At this point it may be easier to determine the order the ideas should be placed in.

Treasure Maps

A major key to attaining any goal is to keep the goal as a dominant thought in your mind. Placing little notes to remind yourself on the bathroom mirror are great but hardly inspiring. I suggest you create a treasure map. For example, let's say your goal is to own a luxurious cabin in the mountains overlooking a lake. To create a treasure map for this goal you would cut out all the pictures of suitable cabins from magazines. In addition, find pictures of lakes, mountains, and woods to simulate what your goal would look like. You can also find pictures for what the interior would look like, the furniture, the roaring fireplace and any other aspect you can imagine.

Take these pictures and glue them to a piece of paper and create a collage of your goal in living color. This treasure map will vividly represent the goal you desire. With a treasure map you will have no trouble visualizing your goal or getting excited and inspired by it.

You can do this technique for your moving out goal or any other goal you have. Good luck, I hope it helps!

APPENDIX B:

STOP!

DO NOT WRITE ON THE FORMS IN THIS SECTION

Within this section of the book, I have provided several forms to help you organize your move. Since you may be using these forms more than once I suggest you make copies of them. Feel free to copy these forms for your personal use. These forms are not for publication or use in any other work. Make any changes appropriate to your situation.

To get full page (8 1/2 X 11) inch copies of these forms send $5.00 to:

**Richardson Publishing,
3983 S. McCarran Blvd.,
Suite 412-A
Reno, NV 89502**

RENTAL LEASE AGREEMENT

Property Name _____

THIS AGREEMENT is entered into this _____ day of _____, 19____, by and between, _____ Apartments ("Lessor")
and _____ ("Resident").

TERM AND PREMISES: 1. Resident leases from Lessor, Apartment No.____, located at_____ together with the personal
property shown on the attached inventory, if any (the "premises") beginning _____, 19____, for a lease term
of _____.

RENT: 2. Monthly rental as follows shall be payable in lawful money of the United States without deduction or offset, and shall be
delivered to Lessor on the first day of each and every month: LANDLORD WILL ACCEPT NO MORE THAN ONE PERSONAL CHECK AS MONTHLY
PAYMENT OF RENT.

MONTHLY RENT

Base Rent:	$ _____
Furniture:	_____
Washer/Dryer:	_____
Carport/Garage:	_____
Other:	_____
TOTAL MONTHLY RENT:	$ _____

Rent shall be paid as follows:

A. $_____ for the period of _____ through _____

B. $_____ for the period of _____ through _____ (second month prorated.)

C. $_____ commencing on the first day of the month of _____ and thereafter on the first
day of each succeeding month.

USE: 3. Resident shall not use the premises for any purpose other than as a private residence for _____ people.
The premises shall be occupied only by the following named persons: _____
_____

Resident shall not permit the use of the premises by any person or persons other than Resident and the above named persons, or sublease to any
person or persons, or assign this Agreement to any person or persons unless the Lessor shall have first consented in writing to such use, sublease or
assignment. Guests shall not be permitted to occupy the premises for more than 10 days.

DEPOSIT: 4. Resident shall deposit with Lessor the sum of $_____. Lessor may use therefrom such amounts as are rea
sonably necessary to remedy Resident defaults under this Agreement, or defaults in the payment of rent, or to repair damages caused by Resident, or
to clean the premises upon termination of tenancy, or in the event Resident fails to return key at end of occupancy term. If used towards rent or
damages Resident agrees to reinstate said total deposit upon receipt of 5 days' written notice. The balance of such deposit, if any, or notice of a
deposit deficiency, if any, shall be mailed to Resident's last known address within 30 days of surrender of the premises in accordance with this Agreement. In the event of any deficiency in Resident's account after such surrender, Resident shall pay the amount of such deficiency forthwith upon the
receipt of notification of such deficiency. Any refund of the deposit shall be made jointly to those persons signing this Agreement as Resident, if more
than one.

DUTIES OF RESIDENT: 5. Resident shall personally occupy the premises. Resident agrees to exercise due care in the use of the premises and to keep all
areas under Resident's control free from dirt, trash and filth. Resident also agrees not to alter or damage the common areas of the property. Resident,
whether or not in actual possession of the premises, shall be liable for all damage to the premises caused or permitted by Resident, Resident's guests
and persons under Resident's control.

_____ **ALTERATIONS & REPAIRS:** 6. Except as provided by law, no repairs, decorating or alterations shall be done by Resident without Lessor's prior written
consent. Resident shall notify Lessor in writing of any repairs or alterations contemplated, and Resident shall immediately notify Lessor in writing
should any plumbing, electrical, mechanical or other equipment or part of the premises become damaged, faulty or in disrepair. Lessor shall have the
right to enter the premises in order to make necessary repairs at any time during normal business hours and upon proper notice. Decorations which
require prior written consent include, but are not limited to, painting, wallpapering, hanging of murals or posters. Window coverings are provided by
Lessor, and no draperies, sunshades, foil or other window coverings visible from the exterior of the premises are permitted.

_____ **COMMUNITY POLICIES:** 7. Lessor reserves the right to promulgate such Community Policies relating to the premises and the adjacent areas as Lessor
may deem appropriate. Resident agrees to abide by such Community Policies and cooperate in their observance. Such Community Policies may be
amended by Lessor from time to time with or without advance notice, and all amendments shall be effective upon posting by Lessor at the office of
the resident manager. Resident acknowledges receipt of a copy of the current Community Policies, a copy of which is attached to their Agreement,
and agrees to be bound thereby.

_____ **UTILITES:** 8. Lessor shall pay all bills for water supplied to the premises and for the routine disposal of garbage. Resident shall pay for all
other utilities and services supplied to the premises, except_____
Lessor shall not be liable to Resident or any other person for damages resulting from the interruption of any utility services provided the premises,
whether due to power outages, shut-off for repair purposes or otherwise.

_____ **FAILURE TO PAY RENT OR OTHER DEFAULT:** 9. The Resident agrees to pay Lessor the sum of $_____ as a late charge if the rent is not
paid in full by the fifth (5) day of the month. There will be a further charge of $_____ per day for each day the rent payment is later
after the fifth (5) of the month. This charge will be assessed each time the rent is not paid when due. If any rent shall be due and unpaid five (5)
days after due, or if default shall be made by Resident in any of the other covenants herein contained, the Lessor, at its option, may terminate Resident's tenancy with proper notice to Resident. Resident also agrees to pay an additional charge of $25.00 for each NSF check received by Lessor. ON
THE 6TH OF EACH MONTH, RENT MUST BE PAID IN THE FORM OF CASHIER'S CHECK OR MONEY ORDER.

_____ **TERMINATION OF RESIDENCY BY RESIDENT:** 10. IF THIS AGREEMENT IS FOR A TERM OF MORE THAN THIRTY (30) DAYS, RESIDENT MAY NOT
TERMINATE THIS LEASE PRIOR TO THE EXPIRATION OF SUCH TERM. FURTHERMORE, RESIDENT MUST GIVE THE RESIDENT MANAGER AT
THE PROPERTY AT LEAST THIRTY DAYS ADVANCE WRITTEN NOTICE OF RESIDENT'S INTENTION TO VACATE THE PREMISES REGARDLESS OF
THE TERM OF TENANCY. Upon request, Lessor will supply forms for the use of Resident to give such notice, and upon request Lessor will give its
written acknowledgement of receipt of such notice to Resident. Resident agrees to pay rent for the entire lease term and, in any event, for thirty days
beyond the date notice of intent to vacate was given. For purposes of prorating rent refunds, a 30 day month shall be presumed, and Resident shall
pay such prorated rent for each day the premises is occupied. Resident agrees to vacate the premises before 6:00 p.m. on the day specified in the
notice as the last day of Resident's occupancy of the premises, and Resident shall be liable for any damages caused by Resident's failure to so vacate.
Any hold-over shall be presumed to be willful and deliberate, and Lessor shall be entitled to treble damages for the holdover period, plus such
other damages Lessor may incur through the loss of a prospective tenant, and other expenses incurred due to breach of this Agreement, including
attorney's fees and costs expended.

130

SO YOU WANT TO MOVE OUT?

ABANDONMENT: 11. Resident's absence from the premises for sixteen (16) consecutive days, while all or any portion of the rent is unpaid, shall be deemed an abandonment of said premises, and in such event the tenancy shall, at the option of Lessor, terminate without further notice. In such event, Lessor may dispose of all resident's property remaining on said premises and re-rent said premises without any liability to Resident in accordance with Nevada law.

TERMINATION OF RESIDENCY OR CHANGE BY OWNER: 12. After expiration of the lease term, this residency may be terminated by Lessor with or without cause, upon thirty (30) days written notice to the Resident.

PARKING: 13. Resident shall be entitled to use and occupy parking space No.____ during the term of the tenancy herein above provided; provided, however, that Lessor reserves the right to alter or modify such parking designation upon five (5) day written notice to Resident. Vehicles shall never be backed into stalls, and shall not be parked so as to interfere with vehicles of other residents. Parking spaces are to be used only for the parking of automobiles, and all parking at the property is subject to the Community Policies.

INSPECTION: 14. In addition to Lessor's right to immediately enter the premises in the event of an emergency, Lessor shall have the right at any and all reasonable times upon proper notice to Resident to enter and inspect the premises, including the right to show the premises to prospective residents for purposes of re-renting after notice of intent to vacate has been given by Resident, or to any and all prospective purchasers, mortgagees, or other persons having a legitimate interest therein, or to inspect for necessary repairs. Lessor also reserves the right to make periodic inspections of the premises to insure that smoke detectors are functional. Resident has inspected the premises, furnishings and equipment, and has found the same to be satisfactory. Resident agrees that all plumbing, heating and electrical equipment is presently operative, and furniture, if any, as inventoried and attached hereto, has likewise been inspected and is deemed satisfactory by Resident.

NUISANCE: 15. Resident shall not keep or permit to be kept in the premises or upon the property any boats, motorcycles, campers, pickup trucks, trailers, old cars, dogs, cats, birds, or other animals or pets unless agreed to in writing by Lessor, nor shall Resident use the premises for any unlawful or immoral purpose, nor shall Resident in any manner disturb, annoy, endanger, or inconvenience any other resident or any other person in the property of which the premises may form a part, nor shall Resident violate nor permit to be violated any Federal, State, County or Municipal law, ordinance, rule or regulation pertaining to the use or occupancy of the premises, nor violate nor permit to be violated the Community Policies.

POSSESSION: 16. If Lessor for any reason connot deliver possession of the premises at the commencement of term as set forth in paragraph 1, Lessor shall not be liable to Resident for any damages resulting therefrom, but there shall be a proportionate deduction of rent. In the event Lessor cannot deliver possession as set forth above, this Agreement shall not be void or voidable for a period of fifteen (15) days after the date set forth in paragraph 1. If, for any reason, the premises cannot be delivered within said number of days, Resident may, at Resident's option declare this Agreement to be null and void, and in such event all money paid to Lessor by Resident shall be refunded to Resident.

PATIO MAINTENANCE: 17. Patio areas may contain patio-type furniture or flower boxes or pots, but no other item may be stored or hung in such area, and no items such as flower pots or other hazard creating itmes may be placed on balcony or stairway railings.

LOCKS: 18. Resident shall not change any lock or place additional locks an any door of the premises without prior written consent of Lessor.

PETS: 19. NO PETS ALLOWED, UNLESS AGREED IN WRITING BY LESSOR AND A PET AGREEMENT IS SIGNED.

WATER BEDS: 20. Water beds and other liquid filled furniture are not permitted in the premises unless by express written permission of Lessor, and, if such permission is given, Resident must sign a waterbed agreement and provide water bed insurance acceptable to Lessor in the amount of at least $100,000.00, which policy shall name Lessor as an additional insured.

NOTICES: 21. All notices by either party to this Agreement shall be in writing. Notice to Resident shall be made by personal delivery or shall be mailed to Resident addressed to the premises postage prepaid. Notice to Lessor shall be made by personal delivery given to the resident manager at the property.

ATTORNEY FEES: 22. In the event of any dispute related to this Lease, the losing party shall pay the prevailing party's actual attorney fees and expenses incurred in any phase of the dispute.

NO LIABILITY FOR LOSS: 23. Resident acknowledges that the premises and the property of which the premises is a part is not a "security" building. Lessor makes no representations nor warranties that the premises are secure from theft or any other criminal activity perpetrated by any resident or others. Security officers to the extent that they may be on the premises and other security facilities provided by Lessor are for the Resident's convenience only, and Lessor makes no warranty or representations as to the effectiveness of any such security officers or facilities as a deterrent against any criminal activity, damage, or injury to Resident or any invitee of Resident, or the personal property of Resident or any invitee of Resident.

BARBECUES: 24. Gas or electric barbecues are permitted to be used at locations in the common areas approved and designated by the office only.

ADDENDUM: 25. By initialling as provided, Resident acknowledges that additional terms and provisions have been agreed upon which are designated as an Addendum, a copy of which is attached hereto and incorporated herein.

JOINT & SEVERAL LIABILITY: 26. Each person executing this Agreement as Resident shall be jointly and severally liable hereunder, whether or not in actual possession of the premises, and each such person is required to perform in full all obligations to be performed by Resident under this Agreement.

MISCELLANEOUS: 27. Resident representations made in the rental application shall be considered inducement to Lessor to execute this Agreement. Misrepresentations in the application shall be considered as cause to terminate this Agreement. Each and every term, covenant and agreement herein contained shall be deemed a condition hereof. No oral agreements have been entered into and this Agreement shall no be modified unless such modification is reduced to writing. Waiver by Lessor of any singular breach of any singular term or singular condition of this Agreement shall not constitute a waiver of subsequent breaches. Time shall be of the essence of this Agreement. The invalidity or partial invalidity of any provision of this Agreement shall not render the remainder of the Agreement invalid or unenforceable.

By: _____   Resident: _____
    Agent for Lessor

     _____

APARTMENT COMPARISON CHECKLIST	APT. #1	APT. #2	APT. #3	APT. #4
CLEAN CARPETING ?				
FRESH PAINT, NO CRACKS IN WALLS ?				
CHECK ALL HARDWARE IN APARTMENT ?				
DOORKNOBS, WINDOWS, FAUCETS, LOCKS				
APPLIANCES WORK PROPERLY ?				
OVEN, STOVE, REFRIGERATOR, TOILET				
# ELECTRICAL OUTLETS PER ROOM ?				
WHAT KIND OF CURRENT ?				
FUSE BOX IN APARTMENT ?				
LIGHTS MOUNTED IN EVERY ROOM ?				
HEATER TYPE ? LAST SERVICE DATE ?				
WATER HEATER CAPACITY ?				
WATER PRESSURE ADEQUATE ?				
CLEAN TILES AND GROUTING ?				
TOILETS AND DRAINS WORK PROPERLY ?				
LAST WATER SAFETY TEST / RESULTS ?				
TRASH AND PAPER COLLECTION ?				
DATE UTILITY METERS ARE READ ?				
EMERGENCY EXITS CLEARLY MARKED ?				
SUFFICIENT LIGHTING IN HALLS ?				
SUFFICIENT LIGHTING OUTSIDE ?				
OCCUPANCY / HEALTH PERMITS NEEDED?				
COVERED PARKING PROVIDED ?				
LOCKED / SECURED STORAGE AREAS ?				
PETS ALLOWED, SIZE LIMITS ?				
CHILDREN ALLOWED, SIZE LIMITS ?				
VISITOR PARKING, WHERE ?				

APARTMENT COMPARISON CHECKLIST	APT. #1	APT. #2	APT. #3	APT. #4
ABILITY TO ADD FIXTURES ?				
INSECT / RODENT EXTERMINATIONS ?				
RADON / METHANE GAS TESTS ?				
DOORS / WINDOWS WEATHER STRIPPED ?				
UTILITY HOOK UPS ACCESSIBLE ?				
LAUNDRY ROOM ?				
SWIMMING POOLS ?				
FITNESS CENTER ?				
TENNIS COURTS ?				
JACUZZI / SAUNA ?				
CLUBHOUSE ?				
CLOSE TO SHOPPING ?				
CLOSE TO TRANSPORTATION ?				
CLOSE TO WORK ?				
MONTHLY RENT AMOUNT ?				
ANY ADDITIONAL COSTS ?				
TYPE / LENGTH OF LEASE ?				
SPECIAL CONSIDERATIONS / OFFERS ?				
SQUARE FOOTAGE OF APARTMENT ?				
NUMBER OF BEDROOMS ?				
AMOUNT OF CLOSET / STORAGE SPACE ?				
COLOR SCHEME IN APARTMENT ?				
BALCONY OR PATIO ?				
WHO CONTROLS HEAT OR AIR ?				
AVERAGE MONTHLY UTILITY COSTS ?				
SECURITY ON PREMISES ?				
ANY DISTINCT ADVANTAGE ?				

APARTMENT COMPARISON CHECKLIST	APT. #1	APT. #2	APT. #3	APT. #4

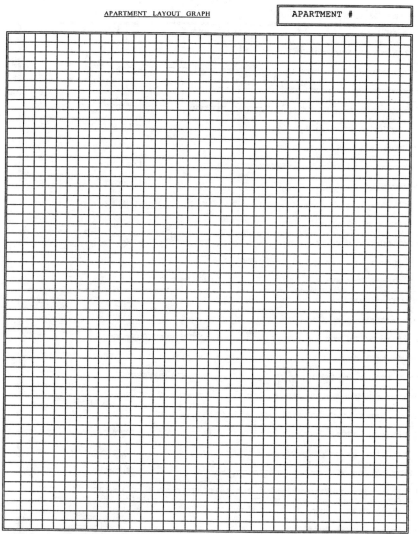

APARTMENT LAYOUT GRAPH

APARTMENT #

USE THIS GRAPH TO MAKE A DRAWING OF THE LAYOUT OF EACH APARTMENT.   INCLUDE
EXITS AND ENTRANCES, CLOSETS, BALCONIES, AND ANY UNIQUE FEATURES.

135

SAMPLE CREDIT / APARTMENT APPLICATION FORM

MOVE IN DATE:	APARTMENT #		TYPE:

FULL NAME OF APPLICANT:

SOCIAL SECURITY #	DATE OF BIRTH:

CURRENT ADDRESS:

CITY:	STATE:	ZIP:	PHONE:

HOW LONG?	LANDLORD:	PHONE:

PREVIOUS ADDRESS:

CITY:	STATE:	ZIP:	PHONE:

HOW LONG?	LANDLORD:	PHONE:

EMPLOYER:	PHONE:

ADDRESS:

POSITION:	SALARY:

HOW LONG?	PREVIOUS EMPLOYER:	PHONE:

ADDITIONAL INCOME:	HOW MUCH?

CREDIT REFERENCES

BANK BRANCH:	PHONE:

CHECKING ACCOUNT #	SAVINGS ACCOUNT #

CREDIT CARD #	CREDIT CARD #

CAR FINANCE COMPANY	MONTHLY PAYMENT:

STORE / GAS CARD:	STORE / GAS CARD:

ADDITIONAL CREDIT INFORMATION:

NEAREST RELATIVE:	PHONE:

ADDRESS:

EMERGENCY CONTACT:	PHONE:

APPLICANT REPRESENTS THE ABOVE INFORMATION IS TRUE TO THE BEST OF HIS/HER KNOWLEDGE AND AUTHORIZES INVESTIGATION AND VERIFICATION OF THE INFORMATION CONTAINED HEREIN.

APPLICANTS SIGNATURE:	DATE:

FOR OFFICE USE ONLY:

Daily Spending Record

Date	Description of Purchase or Payment	Amount Spent	

YEARLY BUDGET

Yearly Income: For the year _____ .		
Salary / Tips		
Bonuses / Commissions		
Outside Sources (Alimony, Royalties, Etc.)		
Interest Income / Dividends		
Benefits (Social Security / Welfare)		
Total Yearly Income:		

Yearly Expenses: For the year _____ .		
Rent / Mortgage		
Insurance: Automobile		
Health / Medical / Life		
Property		
Utilities: (Gas, Electric, Water, Etc.)		
Telephone		
Food		
Transportation -Gas, Tolls, Parking, Repair		
Installment Loans: Automobile		
Furniture		
Other		
Credit Cards		
Savings		
Taxes		
School / Continuing Education		
Hobbies / Entertainment		
Miscellaneous (Birthdays, Holidays, Etc.)		
Total Yearly Expenses:		

Personal Budget - Monthly / Yearly

Yearly / Monthly Income: Month_____ Year_____		
Total Yearly / Monthly Income:		

Yearly / Monthly Expenses: Month_____ Year_____		
Total Yearly / Monthly Expenses:		

(Use this form to create a monthly or yearly budget unique to your needs.)

ANNUAL PAYMENT RECORD

Date	Description of Purchase or Payment	Amount Spent	
	Driver's License Fee		
	Car Registration		
	Car Inspection		
	Smog Inspection for Car		
	Professional Licenses, Fees, or Dues		
	Subscriptions		
	Business Seminars / Clinics		
	Vacations		
	Medical Examinations		
	Taxes (Federal and State)		
	Christmas (gifts, cards, visits)		
	Birthdays		
	Anniversaries		
	Consumer Holidays (Mother's Day, Valentines)		
	Other:		

KITCHEN BASICS

SILVERWARE	BROOM / DUSTPAN
PLATES	ALL PURPOSE CLEANER
BOWLS	POT HOLDERS
CUPS	ALUMINUM FOIL
GLASSES	MOP / BUCKET
ASSORTED COOKING UTENSILS	FLOOR CLEANER
POTS	SPONGE / SCOURING PADS
MICROWAVE COOKWARE	BASIC CONDIMENTS
CAN OPENER	SALT / PEPPER
STRAINER	SUGAR
BAKING PANS	SPICES
TOASTER OVEN / TOASTER	BUTTER / MARGARINE
MICROWAVE OVEN	KETCHUP
BLENDER	MUSTARD
TRASH CAN	MAYONNAISE
KITCHEN TABLE	RELISH
CHAIRS	COFFEE / TEA / HOT CHOCOLATE
REFRIGERATOR	CREAMER
GRILL / BARBECUE	BREAD
MEASURING CUPS	COOKING OIL
NAPKINS	PEANUT BUTTER / JELLY
DISH SOAP	SYRUP
SMOKE DETECTOR	MILK
ICE CUBE TRAYS	EGGS
PAPER TOWELS	SOFT DRINKS
DISH CLOTH / TOWELS	SNACKS
TUPPERWARE	MEATS
TRASH BAGS	FRUITS AND VEGETABLES
PLASTIC WRAP	CEREALS AND DAIRY PRODUCTS

LIVING ROOM / BEDROOM BASICS

LIVING ROOM BASICS:		BEDROOM BASICS:
TELEVISION		BED / FRAME
VIDEO RECORDER / BLANK TAPES		SHEETS
COUCH / CHAIRS		MATTRESS PROTECTOR
LAMPS / LIGHTING		CLOCK / RADIO-CASSETTE
CASSETTE / CD PLAYER		TRASH CAN
BOOKCASE		SMOKE DETECTOR
TV STAND / MAGAZINE RACK		PICTURES / POSTERS
CURTAINS / BLINDS		JEWELRY BOX
PICTURES / POSTERS		PILLOW / PILLOW CASES
COFFEE & END TABLES		BLANKETS / COMFORTERS
COAT RACK		CHEST OF DRAWERS
HOME "WORK" AREA		TABLE LAMP
DESK / TABLE & CHAIR		TABLE / DESK
TELEPHONE		CURTAINS / BLINDS
ANSWERING MACHINE		CHAIR
STATIONERY / ENVELOPES		SUITCASES
STAMPS / PHONE LOG		MIRROR
COMPUTER		HANGERS
PRINTER		CLOSET ORGANIZERS / SHOE TREE
FILING SYSTEM		
RETURN ADDRESS STAMP		
PHONE BOOK		
CALENDAR		
CLOCK		
LAMP / LIGHTING		
APPOINTMENT BOOK		

BATHROOM / LAUNDRY BASICS

BATHROOM BASICS:	TOILET CLEANER
BATH TOWELS	Q-TIPS
HAND TOWELS	COSMETICS
WASH CLOTHS	FEMININE PRODUCTS
BATH MAT	MEDICINES / BIRTH CONTROL
SHOWER CURTAIN (?)	CLOTHING BASICS:
TOILET BRUSH	SHOES / POLISH
RAZOR BLADES	UNDERCLOTHES
TOOTH BRUSH	PANTS
HAIR BRUSH	SHIRTS / BLOUSES
NAIL CLIPPERS	FORMAL WEAR
WEIGHT SCALE	SLEEPWEAR
CLOTHES HAMPER	SKIRTS / DRESSES
TRASH CAN	JACKETS
BLOW DRYER / CURLING IRON	RAINCOAT
NIGHT LIGHT	SPORTS CLOTHES
TOILET PAPER	GLASSES / CONTACTS
FACIAL TISSUES	MEDICAL DEVICES
TUB / TILE CLEANER	LAUNDRY BASICS:
SHAMPOO / CONDITIONER	LAUNDRY BASKETS
SOAP	LAUNDRY DETERGENT
SKIN LOTION	FABRIC SOFTENER
DEODORANT	IRON
SHAVING CREAM	LAUNDRY BAGS
TOOTH PASTE / DENTAL FLOSS	DRYING RACK
HAIRSPRAY	CHANGE FOR MACHINES
MOUTHWASH	HANGERS
PERFUME / COLOGNE	
DISINFECTANT	

PROPER NOTIFICATION / CHANGE OF ADDRESS CHECKLIST

SEND CHANGE OF ADDRESS TO:	TERMINATE THESE SERVICES:
Post Office	Newspaper Delivery
IRS (Federal And State Offices)	Gardener / Housecleaner
Credit Card Companies	Babysitter / Nanny
Attorney	Gas, Electric, Cable TV
Accountant	Telephone
Doctor	Other (Sewer, Trash, Etc.)
Dentist	CLOSE THESE ACCOUNTS:
Veterinarian	Bank (checking, saving, CD's)
Insurance Agent (all types)	Safety Deposit Box
Bank	Local Business Charge Accounts
Credit Union / Finance Co.	Other
Stockbroker	COLLECT THESE RECORDS/DOCUMENTS:
Employer (personnel office)	School Records and Transcripts
Professional Organizations	Dental Records and X-Rays
Clubs (Health, or other)	Medical Records and X-Rays
Subscriptions	Current Prescriptions (refill?)
Selective Service Bureau	Veterinary Records- update shots
Department of Motor Vehicles	Tax Records from Accountant
Church or Synagogue	Legal Documents from Attorney
Friends	W-2's from Employer
Relatives	Letter of Reference from job
Business Colleagues	Other
Voter Registration	TRANSFER / START SERVICES
City / County Tax Assessor	Gas, Electric, Water, Trash
Mom and Dad	Cable TV, newspaper
School / College	Transfer licenses, registration
Significant Other	Professional licenses & Fees
(Any) Other	Other

"I WANT TO MOVE OUT EXPENSE LIST"

Please use this form to list all expenses related to moving
and setting up your first apartment or home.

EXPENSE LIST FOR: LOCATION _____ APT. #_____		
RENT / LEASE: FIRST MONTH		
LAST MONTH		
SECURITY DEPOSIT		
APARTMENT APPLICATION FEES		
UTILITY DEPOSITS: TELEPHONE		
ELECTRIC / GAS / OIL		
WATER / SEWER		
TRASH		
CABLE TELEVISION		
HOUSEHOLD FURNITURE		
BASIC NECESSITIES & SET UP SUPPLIES		
MOVING EXPENSES: PACKING AND SHIPPING		
TRUCK / TRAILER RENTAL		
TOWING GEAR		
CAR CHECK UP / TUNE UP		
GAS / TOLLS / PARKING		
MOTELS / FOOD		
PRE-MOVE INSPECTION?: AIR FARE		
MOTEL / FOOD		
RENTAL CAR		
CHECKING ACCOUNT INITIAL DEPOSIT		
OTHER:		
TOTAL MOVE OUT EXPENSES:		

MOVING EXPENSES LIST

1. TRUCK / TRAILER RENTAL		
2. LIGHTS FOR TRAILER		
3. ADDITIONAL SIDE MIRRORS?		
4. ATTACH TOW BAR		
5. PACKING ITEMS: BOXES		
LABELS, FILLER, TAPE		
SHIPPING FEES?		
6. EQUIPMENT RENTAL:		
DOLLIES, BLANKETS		
PADDING, ROPES		
RAMPS		
7. CAR TUNE UP		
8. TRAILER TO TOW CAR?		
9. DROP OFF FEE ON TRAILER?		
10. EXTRA INSURANCE NEEDED?		
11. GAS, TOLLS, PARKING		
12. FOOD		
13. MOTELS		
14. REPAIRS		
15. AUTO CLUB MEMBERSHIP		
16.		
17.		
TOTAL MOVING EXPENSE		

Please feel free to add to this list any items
you consider to be important in your situation.

MOVING DAY - LAST MINUTE CHECKLIST

	VITAL DOCUMENTS:
	DRIVER'S LICENSE
	CAR REGISTRATION
	INSURANCE VERIFICATION CARD
	RENTAL PAPERS FOR TRAILER
	APARTMENT LEASE
	TRAVEL PLANS / MAPS
	THE FINAL CHECKLIST
	IS EVERYTHING LOADED?
	CLEAR VISIBILITY ON ALL SIDES
	LOAD EVENLY DISTRIBUTED
	ALL LIGHTS WORKING: (BRAKES,
	HEADLIGHTS, TURN SIGNALS,
	PARKING, AND EMERGENCY LIGHTS
	TRAILER HITCHED WITH SAFETY CHAIN
	OKAY, REALLY THE FINAL CHECKLIST!
	CONFIRM ALL RESERVATIONS
	TURN OFF EVERYTHING BEFORE LEAVING
	RECORD UTILITY METER READINGS
	RETURN KEYS TO PARENTS / LANDLORD
	LEAVE ADDRESS, HAVE MAIL COLLECTED
	NOTIFY POLICE OF DEPARTURE
	RECONFIRM TRAVEL PLANS, SAY BYE!

Please feel free to add to this list any items
you consider to be important in your situation.

BASIC TOOLKIT

	Adjustable Pliers
	Crescent Wrenches (U.S. or Metric)
	Adjustable Wrenches
	Phillips Head Screwdrivers
	Flat Head Screwdrivers
	Claw Hammer
	Pocket Knife
	Roll of Duct Tape
	Flashlight
	Spare Fuses for your car
	Aerosol Tire Inflator
	Road Flares
	Get Help sign
	Towelettes to clean up with
	Garbage bags to kneel on

Please feel free to add to this list any items
you consider to be important in your situation.

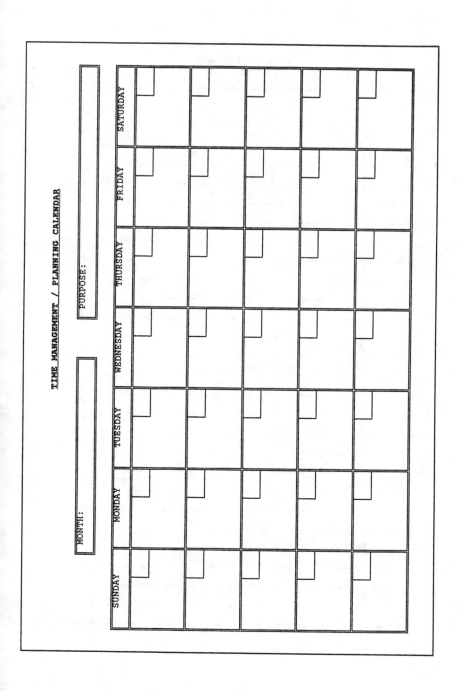

DAILY "TO DO" LIST

DATE / TIME	PROJECT, APPOINTMENT, OR GOAL TO ACCOMPLISH	COMMENTS

PERSONAL ADDRESS FILE

NAME:	

STREET ADDRESS:

CITY:	STATE:	ZIP:
COUNTRY:	AREA CODE & PHONE # ( )	
COMMENTS:		

NAME:	

STREET ADDRESS:

CITY:	STATE:	ZIP:
COUNTRY:	AREA CODE & PHONE # ( )	
COMMENTS:		

NAME:	

STREET ADDRESS:

CITY:	STATE:	ZIP:
COUNTRY:	AREA CODE & PHONE # ( )	
COMMENTS:		

NAME:	

STREET ADDRESS:

CITY:	STATE:	ZIP:
COUNTRY:	AREA CODE & PHONE # ( )	
COMMENTS:		

NAME:	

STREET ADDRESS:

CITY:	STATE:	ZIP:
COUNTRY:	AREA CODE & PHONE # ( )	
COMMENTS:		

NAME:	

STREET ADDRESS:

CITY:	STATE:	ZIP:
COUNTRY:	AREA CODE & PHONE # ( )	

PERSONAL TELEPHONE LOG

Date	Number Called	Person Called / Reason	# Minutes
	( )		
	( )		
	( )		
	( )		
	( )		
	( )		
	( )		
	( )		
	( )		
	( )		
	( )		
	( )		
	( )		
	( )		
	( )		
	( )		
	( )		
	( )		
	( )		
	( )		
	( )		
	( )		
	( )		
	( )		
	( )		
	( )		
	( )		
	( )		
	( )		
	( )		

REFERENCES & SUGGESTED READING

"Move It!: A Guide To Relocating Family, Pets, and Plants"
by Nan DeVincentis Hayes
Copyright 1989
Red Dember Enterprises, Corp.
80 Eighth Ave., NY, NY, 10011

"Moving: Don't Be Taken For An Expensive Ride"
by Henry P. Constantino
Copyright 1988
Transportation Publishing Co.
P.O. Box 2309-B
Mission Viejo, CA 92690

"Positive Moves"
by Carolyn Janik
Copyright 1988
Weidenfeld & Nicholson
Division of Wheatland Corporation
841 Broadway
NY, NY, 10003-4793

"The Handbook For Apartment Living"
by Joan Bingham
Copyright 1981
Chilton Book Co.
Radnor, PA

"Clean Your House And Everything In It"
by Eugenia Chapman and Jill C. Major
Copyright 1982
Grosset & Dunlop
New York

"See You At The Top"
by Zig Ziglar
Copyright 1975, 1977
Pelican Publishing Co.
1101 Monroe St.
Gretna, LA 70053

"The World of Credit"
by David B. Triemert
Papermate Publishing Co.
4320 Atlantic Ave. / Suite 4-A
Long Beach, CA 90807

Employee Relocation Council
1720 N. Street, N.W.
Washington, D.C. 20036
(202) 857-0857

Apartment Rental Book
15 E. Ridge Pike / Suite 340
Conshohocken, PA 19428
(215) 834-1234
(800) 275-8158

United Services Automobile Association
USAA Building
San Antonio, TX
(800) 531-8111

Apartment Relocation Council
Guidebook Request
5664 Peachtree Rd.
Atlanta, GA 30341
(800) 232-RENT

Shared Housing Resource Center
6344 Greene Street
Philadelphia, PA 19144

Awaken The Giant Within
by Anthony Robbins
Copyright 1991
Summit Books
Rockefeller Center
1230 Avenue of the Americas
NY, NY 10020

Consumer Information Center
Department 71
Pueblo, CO 81009

Consumer Affairs /Housing
1909 K Street NW
Washington, DC 20049

Consumer Credit Counseling
1-800-275-0137

Equifax
1-800-685-1111

The Official Rules
by Paul Dickson
Copyright 1978
Dell Publishing Company, Inc.
1 Dag Hammarskjold Plaza
New York, NY 10017

ORDERING INFORMATION:

To Get a copy of:

"So You Want To Move Out?: A Guide To Living On Your Own"

send $14.95 plus $3.00 shipping and handling to:

RICHARDSON PUBLISHING
3983 S. McCarran Boulevard
Suite 412-A
Reno, NV 89502

Richardson Publishing also publishes special reports that may be of interest to anyone getting ready to move out. To receive a copy of:

"The Basics Of Cooking On A Budget"
or
"How To Buy A Car"

send $6.00 for an individual report or $10.00 for both plus $2.00 shipping and handling to Richardson Publishing at the address listed above. Please specify which report you would like.

For credit card orders, or to order by phone call:

1-800-352-6657